STEEL ON STEEL

STEEL ON STEEL

Inside the battle for the future of Australia's biggest railroad

STEPHEN BAINES

UQP

First published 2014 by
Custom Publishing,
University of Queensland Press,
PO Box 6042, St Lucia,
Queensland 4067, Australia.

Custom publisher: Lynn P Bryan
Designer: Avril Makula
Editor: Janet Hutchinson
Copy editor: Puddingburn, Sydney

www.uqp.com.au

ISBN 978-0-7022-5349-2

Cataloguing-in-Publication entry is available from the National Library of Australia
http://catalogue.nla.gov.au

Printed in China.

Front cover: Photograph by Steffan Jannides.

MIX
Paper from
responsible sources
FSC® C016973

CONTENTS

FOREWORD

After my first meeting with Queensland Rail (QR) CEO Lance Hockridge in Montreal in 2009, I wondered if this thoughtful, mild-mannered gentleman was going to survive the bruising gauntlet he was about to face in trying to privatise QR.

In retrospect, it is clear that only someone with his tact, tenacity and steely strength could have succeeded.

Fourteen years before this meeting, as Canadian Transport Minister, I had been at the helm of the commercialisation of Canada's government-owned railroad, Canadian National. While the CN privatisation was a major challenge, I have to say that it was a cakewalk compared to the QR/Aurizon journey.

In the case of QR, one would have thought that widely documented earlier experiences in New Zealand, Great Britain, Canada as well as in Australia would have served as examples to those who were interested in the process and outcomes of previous privatisations.

Yet I have never seen such an extraordinary and relentless counter-attack on a necessary and worthwhile government reform.

It should not come as any surprise that the QR proposal would be seen as a threat by the leaders of rail unions. Their reaction and rejection was similar to attempts in any sector to bring about substantial change. And certainly the position taken by opposition politicians was equally understandable and consistent with political reality.

But the reaction from mining companies, other governments, media, and the investment community added a completely new dimension to the opposition.

Only the resolve of Andrew Fraser, the Treasurer in the Queensland Government, and the total commitment and steadfast determination of Hockridge and his team kept the process on the rails.

Stephen Baines, Advisor to the Chair and CEO of QR/Aurizon, enjoyed a singular opportunity to be both a participant and an observer of the QR journey from concept to IPO. His account reveals the lengths that some elements went to in order to thwart government policy and how key players withstood the massive anti-privatisation campaign.

Premier Bligh and her government showed political courage in coming to the decision to privatise QR. The necessity to sell off most of the QR freight operations was the best way to leave behind a taxpayer-supported, bloated, feather-bedded entity and ensure that a crucial component of the transportation infrastructure supporting the Queensland and Australian economies would become a world-class, results-driven, shareholder rail company.

As more and more governments recognise their role is to provide for education, health care, welfare and justice for their citizens, they will continue to take steps to have the private sector be responsible for freight railroads, ports, airports, airlines and air navigation systems based on the concept of user-pays.

As in any complicated, controversial venture there are lessons to be learned. Stephen Baines has written a valuable addition to the very limited literature available that tells the story of a successful government privatisation.

It was one of the most exciting and challenging experiences in my career to play a small part in what has become the most successful government IPO in Australian history.

Hon M Douglas Young PC QC
Former Canadian Minister for Transport
Tracadie, New Brunswick, Canada, May 2014

INTRODUCTION

Since 2007, I have had the privilege of being on the inside to witness and participate in one of the most extraordinary transformations in the history of Australian business.

An icon that touched every part of life in Queensland, QR was famously and audaciously catapulted into the private sector in 2010 after more than 140 years of government ownership.

This is the story of how that big idea was conceived and executed in the face of unprecedented outrage and opposition.

QR was big, but it was slowly and methodically dying. Even though tens of billions of dollars of annual export revenue travelled on its infrastructure, it was not run as a business. Governments expected involvement in daily commercial decisions, customers expected sweet-heart deals, and employees expected jobs for life. With Asciano, a powerful and impressive private competitor on the scene, QR was just never going to survive long-term as a government entity. But thousands, including powerful decision-makers, were in denial. It was the blistering reality of the global financial crisis that blew away this nostalgic luxury.

The two main players in this story, the remarkable chief executive officer (CEO) of QR/Aurizon Lance Hockridge and Queensland's relentless former Treasurer Andrew Fraser, shared that insight and were joined in steely determination to see the process through.

The privatisation of QR was the second biggest in Australian history, and the most difficult. It involved simultaneously a massive de-merger from the passenger rail business, and a $4.6 billion initial public offering (IPO). For

18 months, QR's IPO was Australia's ultimate corporate soap opera. One day it was dead, the next it was full steam ahead. Powerful forces and big-name business and political stars clambered on to the stage, and we found ourselves battling on several fronts at the same time. There was a daily media smorgasbord of rumour, intrigue, speculation and high farce.

Despite these pressures and provocations, the QR privatisation team was never defeatist. Fervently believing in the value of the opportunity we were creating, we may have bled with each hit, but we always picked ourselves up and fought on.

In the end, Aurizon, as it is now known, was saved by the world. It was a Canadian example, the privatisation of Canadian National, which showed people how a government-owned railroad could be a private sector engine of prosperity and growth. And while Australian investors fled the QR float, spooked by negative media and a lack of understanding of railroad value, seasoned international investors enthusiastically embraced the new listing.

I hope that this book can be an inspiration to other back-room operatives such as me. You can make a difference. It is extraordinary what a team can achieve when there is a clear focus, and leaders give their people real belief and a license to do the impossible.

In my case, Aurizon's chair John Prescott and new CEO Lance Hockridge removed all the barriers for me in 2007. They created a new position in which I was dared to think about the future and fire ideas into an ongoing and intimate conversation with them. With no technical knowledge or significant management experience, my only distinction was a creative and quirky mind. How many chairs or CEOs take that sort of risk?

Yet both Prescott and Hockridge knew from decades of business experience that diverse teams make the best decisions. And as our privatisation opportunity unfolded, and then we fought for our very existence, I found myself at the epicentre, and our team's collective creativity was a telling factor in our success.

We are in an era of renewed interest in privatisation and transformation, and clearly the turnaround of QR has influenced what people now believe is possible.

I hope that the successes and the mistakes outlined in the pages of this book provide invaluable lessons for companies and governments who are seeking to do similarly courageous things.

Looking back on the adventure, I think that mostly we made the right calls, although at the time it was sometimes hard to know. For the major decisions, we were guided by a clear principle to set the company up for success, which drove us to fight for an integrated structure, preserve our quality people and protect our important assets. Even our critics would agree that a strong and resilient company has been created.

Privatisation of large government assets can be controversial, and is often difficult to implement. But for many government-owned entities, it should be a simple and compelling proposition. Activities that belong more logically in the commercial sector should not be owned and controlled by governments. We need to allow both companies and people the freedom to be the best that they can be.

Welcome to *Steel on Steel*.

Date	Event
1 July 2006	John Prescott appointed as Chair of QR Limited by the Queensland Government.
30 July 2007	QR accepts recommendations from the O'Donnell review of the Queensland coal system. Announces plans to order new wagons and locomotives.
13 September 2007	Queensland Labor Premier Peter Beattie steps down in favour of his deputy Anna Bligh. Premier Bligh appoints Andrew Fraser as Queensland Treasurer.
8 November 2007	Lance Hockridge appointed as CEO QR Limited.
21 March 2009	Premier Bligh leads Labor to a convincing win in the Queensland State election.
28 April 2009	Hockridge presents QR privatisation proposal to Treasurer Fraser.
2 June 2009	Premier Bligh announces $15 billion program of asset sales to address growing budget deficit. The QR coal business is expected to raise more than a third of the total proceeds.
10-21 August 2009	Hockridge and Stephen Baines travel to Europe and North America to investigate rail privatisations. In Canada they meet with key players behind the successful privatisation of Canadian National.
September 2009	Former head of the Australian Competition and Consumer Commission (ACCC) Allan Fels completes a study into the structural options for a privatised QR.
October 2009	Fels delivers a report focussing on specific issues in the Queensland coal network.
November 2009	Phone conference between Premier Bligh and Paul Martin, the former Canadian Prime Minister.
8 December 2009	Premier Bligh announces that the privatisation of QR National would involve a vertically integrated IPO, to be completed by the end of 2010.
11 December 2009	Queensland Coal Industry Rail Group (QCIRG) delivers a formal offer to buy the Queensland coal network.
9 March 2010	Fourteen coal companies officially launch the QCIRG bid after a meeting in Brisbane.
27 April 2010	Premier Bligh announces new 'blue-chip' board of directors for QR National.
18 May 2010	Asciano announces it has applied to have the Queensland coal network placed under federal regulatory control.
26 May 2010	QCIRG announces they have secured full financing for their bid.
Late May 2010	First IPO pre-marketing roadshow in North America, Europe and Asia. North American investors in particular impressed by the opportunity.
17 June 2010	Premier Bligh applies to the National Competition Council (NCC) for the certification of the Queensland Rail Access Regime as an effective access regime.

Date	Event
22 June 2010	QR fined $600,000 for breaching workplace laws by failing to properly consult the workers over its privatisation plans. Fine is later reduced on appeal.
28 June 2010	ACCC gives interested parties three weeks to submit a response with any competition concerns over the QCIRG bid.
1 July 2010	QR National, the freight entity set for privatisation, is formally separated from Queensland Rail, which will remain in government ownership.
July 2010	Second QR National pre-marketing roadshow in North America, Europe and Asia.
9 August 2010	ACCC suspends the timeline for reviewing the QCIRG bid, seeking further information from the coal companies.
9 August 2010	QCIRG increases bid to $5.2billion on the proviso that they be allowed due diligence within two weeks.
11 August 2010	Hockridge receives a call from the Treasurer to inform him that QCIRG would be allowed to conduct due diligence on the Central Queensland coal network.
7 September 2010	Premier Bligh reiterates the government is seriously considering the QCIRG bid.
9 September 2010	QCIRG withdraws its bid for the Queensland coal network.
14 September 2010	NCC releases a draft recommendation that the Queensland Rail Access Regime be certified as effective for a period of 10 years. The NCC also recommends that the Queensland coal network not be declared.
September 2010	QR National roadshow travels to four continents, holds 171 formal meetings with investors, and interacts with more than 2,000 potential prospects.
1 October 2010	Queensland Competition Authority (QCA) approves QR Network's third access undertaking (UT3).
12 October 2010	Premier Bligh and Treasurer Fraser announce that QR National will float on 22 November 2010.
20 November 2010	Treasurer Andrew Fraser announces QR National will float at $2.45 a share for retail investors and Queenslanders, and $2.55 a share for institutions.
22 November 2010	QR National floats on the Australian Securities Exchange. It closes on its first day of trading at $2.65 — 10 cents above the institutional issue price.
24 March 2012	Campbell Newman and the Liberal National Party win a landslide Queensland election victory over the Labor Party.
8 October 2012	The Queensland Government further reduces its shareholding in QR National with a $1.5 billion buy-back/cornerstone investor placement. QR National shares close up 5.2 per cent on the day.
1 December 2012	QR National changes its name to Aurizon.

PROLOGUE

This was it. There was nowhere to hide for the QR National board and senior executives. A confusing jumble of numbers danced on the wall of a Sofitel conference room in Brisbane. Television cameras and Australian Securities Exchange (ASX) executives studied our faces in the seconds leading up to the float that no-one had expected to happen. Four million shares were for sale at $2.30, or was that someone wanting to buy? Ten million at $2.40 ... then in a spilt second all the numbers were different. A chaotic mix of buyers and sellers jostling for position like sheep bumbling through a farm gate. Three, two, one.

'Welcome to the market,' said the man from the ASX.

Applause rang out, but the price immediately dipped, as did our hearts and stomachs, before rising like a colossus. Within two minutes, it was $2.60, 15 cents above the retail issue price. The confident predictions of a day one crash were proved false. One of the most controversial privatisations in Australian history was proudly afloat.

CHAPTER ONE

Opting in

Proserpine is a sleepy town in North Queensland, home to just over 4,000 people, and dominated by the Proserpine Sugar Mill. The Latin name for the Greek fertility goddess Persephone, Proserpine only occasionally lives up to its billing as a centre of youth, growth and abundance, although it is the gateway to the spectacular Whitsunday tourist region. By grooming Andrew Fraser, the youngest Queensland Treasurer since 1915, however, the town of 'new life' was to underpin an upheaval that would impact on just about every community in the State.

Fraser was academically gifted, although he was beaten to the dux award at the Proserpine State School by his good mate Tom Perkins. He did win the coveted Student of the Year award however, due to his all-round interests. Active in community work during his school years, he was also a keen sportsman, despite his non-Schwarzenegger physique.

In 1992, he was to discover his career passion. Aged 16, he won a week-long trip to Federal Parliament in Canberra, and returned hooked, a committed political junkie. 'He came back very determined about what he was going to do,' Perkins told *The Brisbane Times*. 'He'd go home at lunchtime to watch political shows and everyone would tell him he'd be Prime Minister one day.'[1]

Like many country people, Fraser had a natural curiosity about what was happening beyond his front door. To him, involvement in community and society was part of being human.

'In a smaller town, you have to actively opt out of being involved in the community,' Fraser says. 'Whereas in the urban context, you have to actively opt in to be involved in civic affairs. So politics was the logical extension of being involved in the community where I grew up. But it wasn't in the life plan to be a candidate at 26 and a Minister before the age of 30.'

Fraser secured degrees in commerce and law while working as a budding political staffer for the Australian Labor Party (ALP). He spent time in the office of former Queensland Treasurer David Hamill, and then worked with Queensland Premier Peter Beattie. Beattie went on to become a 'muscular mentor'.

'Despite two unsuccessful attempts to escape his mentoring, Peter spoke to me in 2003 and told me the seat where I lived was about to become vacant,' Fraser says. 'The door's opening and if you're good enough, you're old enough.'

Fraser won ALP pre-selection for the seat of Mount Coot-tha and was elected to the Queensland Parliament in 2004, aged 28.

In Fraser's maiden speech, he surprised with an ability to write, a sharp wit, and a remarkable literary grasp. Within his first five minutes in the House, Fraser had referred to *The Unconscious Civilisation* by John Ralston Saul, the Herman Hesse classic *The Glassbead Game*, and the influential Australian play by Hannie Rayson *Hotel Sorrento*.

Public service, he told the Queensland Parliament, was not an end in itself.

'This can never be the extent of one's endeavour,' said the new member. 'I recall a certain former parliamentary leader in our country declaring that, ultimately, leadership is about doing what is right, not what is popular.'

In 2006, just two years after Fraser entered parliament, his 'muscular mentor' elevated him to the ministry, handing him the complex Local

Government portfolio. In this role, he took on the unenviable task of managing the controversial rationalisation of local councils in Queensland. Fraser impressed both sides of politics with his bias for action, and ability to stare down critics. The issue prompted the biggest street protest in Brisbane since the Vietnam War, and became a live Federal Election issue in 2007.

Premier Beattie and Minister Fraser were pilloried by the State Opposition, the Prime Minister, John Howard, and the Federal Labor Opposition Leader, Kevin Rudd. In what would be a common refrain for Fraser's political life, opponents directly attacked his age and apparent inexperience. Then State Opposition Leader Jeff Seeney was particularly direct, claiming that Fraser was merely 'Peter Beattie's puppet'.

'Peter Beattie made the decision and then he ran away and left a boy to do a man's job,' Seeney told the ABC in May 2007.[2]

Many were underestimating both Fraser's resolute focus on a stated goal, and his appetite for battle. In the media cauldron that followed, Fraser's uncompromising language made it clear that Queensland had found a new conviction politician.[3] Fraser also was using every opportunity to display his gift for florid metaphor.

'We had a Model T and now we have a Ferrari,' he expounded.[4]

Fraser pressed on, in the face of all of the amalgamation opponents, and led the process to implementation, losing just a little skin on the way through (the Noosa Council fought a high-profile rearguard action to preserve their jurisdiction). On the flagship issue of council amalgamation, where doing nothing was not an option, Fraser had earned his spurs.

In 2007, Premier Beattie stepped down and his deputy, Anna Bligh, took over the top job. To the surprise of many, Bligh appointed Andrew Fraser as Treasurer, on the back of very limited ministerial experience.

If there was any lingering modesty or self-doubt, it did not show. In his first press conference as Treasurer, Fraser mistakenly referred to himself as the Premier!

············

Tenterfield, in Northern New South Wales, is as bucolic as Proserpine, with its 3,000 strong population focussed mainly on agriculture. Its most famous sons were the global music star Peter Allen, and the local saddler that Allen immortalised in his hit 'Tenterfield Saddler'.

'I knew the Saddler – I think everyone in Tenterfield did,' recalls Lance Hockridge. 'And my mum's cousin was Peter Allen. That really underlines what a close-knit place it is.'

Lance Edwin Hockridge was born in Tenterfield in 1954. Like Proserpine, Tenterfield gave its inhabitants room to be adventurous, knowing that there was a sympathetic community to provide support if trouble struck.

Brisbane was the nearest city, and the Hockridge family would travel there twice a year, and to Sydney once every couple of years. Hockridge's most vivid early memories were of the trips to Sydney, which, 'when the roads improved', would take 12 to 14 hours.

So although Hockridge enjoyed a typical country upbringing, he was not unfamiliar with the big smoke. Instead of feeling intimidated by the bigger cities, he found them exciting.

Hockridge's grandfather, on his mother's side, was a prospector who 'lobbed into Tenterfield from parts unknown' to participate in a mini gold rush. The family, unremarkably for this region, developed a strong bond with agriculture. One Hockridge uncle ran a sheep property; another a mixed dairy enterprise.

'I don't think you can live in a farming community and not learn resilience,' Hockridge says. 'Making your way through the bad years is very tough. So the main things you learn are resilience, the importance of hard work and that it's up to you to make your way in the world.'

Hockridge found an interest, the Scouts, in which he was able to immerse himself completely. One of the few early Google references to Lance Hockridge is his Queen's Scouts Medal from 1971. He ended up travelling to Japan for the World Scout Jamboree, single-handedly raising the funds to pay for it.

Hockridge's father was from Sydney, and was a carpenter by trade. When Hockridge was sixteen, the family moved to the even sleepier town (population 600) of Bonalbo where his father took up the challenge of running the local ambulance service.

But rather than being cast adrift in a land of inaction and mediocrity, Hockridge was to have a life-changing experience in Bonalbo. He attended a tiny local school that was blessed with a team of high quality teachers.

'The then school principal taught us economics, and also had an interest in industrial relations,' Hockridge says. 'There were only six kids in the whole senior school, and the attention I got was extraordinary.'

Although the young Hockridge thought he would wind up as a lawyer or a member of the foreign service, he chose instead while attending the University of NSW to focus on economics, industrial relations and psychology.

In the mid 1970s, while still at university, Hockridge developed an interest in local politics in inner-western Sydney. He was drawn into a highly charged political atmosphere because of increasing concern about the power of party machines. In July 1980, the nation had been shocked when a left-wing ALP reformer Peter Baldwin, was brutally attacked in his home in Marrickville. Photographs of his battered face hit the front pages and triggered a new movement for change.

A group of like-minded reformists, including Hockridge (now in his late twenties) and a main street pharmacist from Petersham, decided to nominate as independents in the upcoming elections for the then Labor-controlled Marrickville Council.

'We thought there had to be a better way,' Hockridge says. 'This was a local council, not heavy-duty politics. We thought the focus should have been on outcomes for people, rather than the needs of a party machine.'

In the end, all the resources of the Labor party apparatus were trained on the rebels. The mavericks were outspent, out-doorknocked, and outmanoeuvred.

'It was like looking up the hill at this bloody great D9 coming down at you,' Hockridge says.

Hockridge ended up with only a small per centage of the vote, and needless to say, the Marrickville Council remained a Labor fiefdom. But he never lost the appetite for seemingly 'impossible' challenges.

In the meantime, Hockridge had turned his mind to a commercial career. He responded to a routine advertisement for an industrial officer with Australia's largest company, the industrial giant BHP, applied and was offered a position. Just three days after joining, he met John Prescott, who was to have a huge influence over his career. Prescott, who would go on to become BHP's CEO, and would much later take on the reins as chair of QR, was at the time an operations manager for BHP Transport.

. . . .

The combination of John Prescott and Lance Hockridge, both in the formative BHP years and during the creation of QR National/Aurizon, is a most unusual one in the heavy industrial world. Both are from the 'softer' side of the academic street. The lesson for Hockridge has been to retain the insights and instincts of the more people-oriented disciplines, while surrounding himself with technical subject matter experts who ensure that businesses operate efficiently.

'In the old days, if there was going to be somebody other than from the line make it to the top it would be from finance,' Hockridge says. 'So to that extent the change is reflective of what the world has learned over the last 25 to 30 years or so. The differentiating factor between good and great businesses is the human side of things.'

BHP in the late 1970s was a perfect laboratory to learn about the psychology of industrial relations. The company was still very much steel-related, even though an embryonic minerals business was emerging. Hockridge moved into the shipping and stevedoring side of the business at a time when the industrial landscape was at its most volatile.

'The power of the unions was at extraordinary levels,' he recalls. 'Everything was tipped their way. I came face to face with names that are now part of industrial folklore. Charlie Fitzgibbon, Elliott V Elliott, Tas Bull, Pat Geraghty – the movement was controlled by the communists, which was an enormous challenge.'

Hockridge was fortunate to learn from some of the masters, like then Manager, Industrial Relations, John Sullivan, who brought integrity and capability to everything he did.

What is remarkable is the respect, bordering on affection, he holds for the union combatants of the era.

'These guys meant what they said. If you ever shook hands with any of them on a deal, you knew it would stick,' Hockridge says.

This was all useful experience for the young man, and helped him hone skills in understatement, control and diplomacy that would prove invaluable in later years.

After a period as head of human resources for BHP Transport, and then operations manager, Hockridge took on the challenge of leading the transport business from 1991 to 1995, a period which included a new wave of waterfront reform.

In 1997, when Prescott was CEO of BHP, Hockridge was offered the monumental challenge of overseeing the closure of the iconic BHP steelworks in Newcastle. Two and a half thousand employees were to lose their jobs.

'Lance was chosen because he had an all-round capability, including an ability to build a common purpose with the workforce,' Prescott recalls.

The comprehensive and meticulous closure plan was implemented over two years from 1997 to 1999. Despite the emotional impact on all involved, Hockridge looks back on the difficult episode with a sense of achievement.

'It was the largest closure of an industrial site in the southern hemisphere and it was done without any industrial disruption,' he recalls. 'We also successfully transitioned to a new long products business. Notwithstanding the emotion of the time, the safety performance of the plant in the last three months was the best in the entire history of the operation.'

Hockridge also instituted a successful 'Pathways' program that managed the transition for the affected employees. This program built on considerable preparation work by a trio of BHP luminaries – President, Long Products, Bob Kirby and two members of his team, Manager, Workplace Relations, Bill Gately and Head of Human Resources, Steve Keogh.

'Our job was to bring all of that work together, in the context where some of the politicians had gone into grandstanding mode,' Hockridge says. 'Which wasn't terribly helpful, I have to say.'

'Notwithstanding the publicity, the job at hand was to work with the employees and with their local union representatives and that's what we did.'

In late 1999, Hockridge moved on to his next assignment with BHP – turning around the Port Kembla steel operation. Inevitably, he brought some baggage with him from the Newcastle closure. Labelled as the 'toe-cutter' in State and Federal parliament, Hockridge hit back.

'My response was, my goal is to ensure the success and longevity of this business and if that means we've got to do tough things, then I'm not going to leave anything undone that has to be done.'

BHP did not shut Port Kembla, but it was radically reformed, along with the rest of the company's steel operations. The reforms led to the creation of a two new Australian steel companies. Onesteel was listed on the ASX in October 2000, and included the reshaped long products division, the downstream market mills and other steel distribution businesses. Bluescope Steel ultimately emerged when the rest of the BHP steel business was spun off into a separate company after BHP's merger with South African mining house Billiton in 2001. Hockridge became a senior executive within Bluescope and in 2004 was offered the opportunity of running the North American business from its headquarters in Dallas.

············

Two key events stand out from Hockridge's tenure as President of North American Operations for Bluescope Steel. The first was a program of radical change that he led at the business, which included some aggressive M&A moves, like the 2004 acquisition of the Butler Manufacturing Company, the world's largest provider of pre-engineered metal building systems. The second was a strong personal involvement in an international trade case affecting BHP Steel.

For a number of years, BHP Steel had supplied slab and hot rolled coil products from its Port Kembla plant to customers on the West Coast of the USA. In March 2002, the ground rules for this business suddenly changed. In response to chronic financial problems in the local steel sector, the US Government imposed a punitive 30 per cent tariff on the majority of steel imported to the US. Canadian and Mexican steel companies were not automatically subjected to the tariff, because they were treated as special cases under the North American Free Trade Agreement (NAFTA). But Australia, and the Port Kembla product, were caught in the net.

For the best part of 18 months, over several extended visits to Washington DC, Hockridge argued his case before the US trade authorities. After a massive advocacy and negotiation effort, and intensive collaboration with senior Australian diplomats in Washington together with BHP Steel's US customers, Hockridge and his team succeeded in convincing the US administration to grant a tariff exemption for the Port Kembla product.[5]

On the strength of this experience, Hockridge would go on to play an active role in the negotiations for the US-Australia Free Trade Agreement, which formally came into effect on 1 January 2005.

Nailing the trade case challenge showed that BHP had created a very good business strategist, but also an experienced diplomat and relationship-builder.

Although Hockridge is a private person, he and wife Suzanne had successfully built up a strong circle of friends in Dallas. The Hockridge home was frequently opened up to functions for customers and employees. Hockridge, Suzanne, and their two children Téa and Christian, managed a vibrant home life despite the intense work pressures of Hockridge's role. It is a fine balancing act that he continues with Aurizon today.

The decision to leave Bluescope was difficult for Hockridge. The company, in its current and previous forms, had been a central part of his working life. The two triggers for his departure were his unsuccessful bid for the Bluescope CEO role (Paul O'Malley became the new company head), and an intriguing leadership offer from the Deep North.

CHAPTER TWO

Last off the rank

The spiky maroon QR logo was everywhere in Queensland. On the trains that took people to work in Brisbane and other regional cities. On the uniforms of freight rail workers throughout the state. On the major buildings in many Queensland regional towns. Queensland Rail (QR) was, and in its new incarnation still is, a dominant presence and driver for many local economies in regional Queensland. In 2010, more than 15,000 Queenslanders were employed by QR, with many more indirectly dependent on it.

If anything seemed off limits to major reform or god-forbid privatisation, it was QR.

According to Paul Cronin,[6] who was in the Corporate Affairs hot-seat at QR before privatisation, even Labor Party insiders were shocked when QR was targeted in the asset sale process. QR's main locations (Ipswich, Rockhampton,

Mackay, Bowen, Townsville) were universally considered Labor heartland. For a Labor Government, decisions didn't come any bigger than this.

'If you'd asked me in 2008 if this could ever happen, I would have said no,' Cronin says. 'A privatisation of something so steeped in Queensland history, in Labor tradition, in employee issues – I would have said you're crazy.'

QR was untouchable for many reasons, not least of all because it appeared that a decision-making veto was held by trade unions – courtesy of both their influence on government, and their dominance of QR.

'We're a heavily unionised workforce, more than 90 per cent,' Cronin says. 'Even our past CEOs were members of the union. In the past, you couldn't be a CEO of QR if you hadn't come up through the ranks.'

Added to the political degree of difficulty was a disdain about the value of the QR assets.

Keith De Lacy,[7] another former Treasurer in the Labor Government and now a director of several companies, admits that as Treasurer he never seriously considered QR for sale. De Lacy remembers the then CEO of Mount Isa Mines (MIM), Nick Stump, challenging him about QR.

'He came in and started banging on about upgrading the Mount Isa to Townsville line,' De Lacy says. 'And I said to him, 'Look, I'll do a deal with you, Nick. I'll sell you the whole Queensland Rail network for a dollar, and you can do what you like with it.' And that's when he faced up to the fact that it was hardly an asset that people wanted'.

De Lacy led a process to make all government enterprises more productive and commercial. But as with many Queensland Government reform programs of the past, selling any part of QR was not a serious option.

So how did things change so dramatically? The seeds of revolution were sown many years before, in much earlier days of coal expansion in Queensland. The history of coal in Queensland is a complicated story of expansion and success, coupled with tension and misalignment. One of the enduring sources of friction was rail, and in particular, a government-owned corporation known as Queensland Rail.

The first phases of growth were relatively smooth. In the 1950s, when Sir Leslie Thiess[8] developed the first commercial scale coal mine at Moura in Central Queensland, Queensland found a rail solution. At the time, there was no direct rail corridor to the logical destination port of Gladstone. So a 'short line' was constructed to join up with the existing coastal line so the coal could get to Gladstone, albeit via an extremely circuitous route.

The Utah Construction and Mining Company created the next step when it signed a major metallurgical coal supply agreement with Japanese trading company Mitsubishi in 1965. This partnership later expanded into a joint venture between the two companies that would unlock quality inland deposits of metallurgical coal in the Bowen Basin in Central Queensland. The breadth of the new venture was astonishing – Utah's franchise covered a 6,330 square kilometre area in the minerals-rich Blackwater region.

The success of Utah led the way for other companies and, by the 1970s, coal mining was a major growth sector in Central Queensland. From a population of just 300 in the early 1960s, the towns of Blackwater, Moranbah and Dysart had swelled to 13,000 inhabitants by the mid-1970s.

The Utah-Mitsubishi joint venture then went through two significant ownership changes. Utah was acquired by General Electric (GE) in 1976 and in 1984, BHP, fast on its way to becoming the world's largest mining company, bought Utah from GE for $2.42 billion, at the time the largest single trading transaction in Australian history.

The impact of this growth on the rail sector was phenomenal. In 1985, Queensland hit a coal haulage mark of 50 million tonnes per year for the first time. By 1999, the 100 million tonnes a year milestone was reached, and just six years later, the network hit the 150 million tonne mark.

From the 1980s, it was Queensland Government policy that coal should be carried by rail, and it invested heavily in the rail network, and key ports. A potent symbol of this commitment was the construction of a massive new coal terminal at Dalrymple Bay in Central Queensland in 1983. The mining companies contributed substantial funding to Government coffers to fuel growth. Royalties, the fees that mining companies paid the State for mining coal, were built into the rail freight rate. In addition, the mining companies made parallel investments in support infrastructure, including full-service mining towns. Everyone was happy until commodity prices started to slide.

Deb O'Toole, the incredibly energetic Irishwoman who would eventually become QR's chief financial officer (CFO) before privatisation, was watching this from the other side of the fence at MIM,[9] and noticed a major change in mining industry attitudes.

'The government had required the companies to build towns all over Queensland, gold-plated infrastructure,' she says. 'But commodity prices didn't go where they were expected, the government didn't change their position and QR was vilified because it was one of the instruments of government. I remember the mining company CEOs, led by Bruce Watson of MIM, marching down George Street as if they were unionists.'

Entering this fray in the early 1980s was the man who would ultimately become chair of QR in 2006, BHP stalwart, John Prescott. Utah, some time before their acquisition by BHP, asked Prescott for advice on how to bring down the rail freight rates in Queensland. Prescott argued the case directly with the then Queensland 'Minister for Everything' Russ Hinze and Queensland Premier, Joh Bjelke-Petersen.

'Joh was totally dismissive,' Prescott says. 'As far as he was concerned, the companies had agreed to the freight rates and therefore they didn't have a paddle. And that was basically it.'

A few years later, after BHP had acquired Utah, Prescott was asked to have another 'go' at reducing the Queensland rail freight rates. 'It was equally successful,' he says.

Although freight rate reform was slow, QR was making progress on other issues. Valiant efforts were made to dismantle the bloated QR cost structure and remove some of the worst inefficiencies. There were significant workforce reductions during the reigns of CEOs Vince O'Rourke (1991 to 2000) and Bob Scheuber (2000 to 2007).

O'Rourke had occasional notable political allies in his quest for change. For example, considerable political courage was shown by Labor Transport Minister, David Hamill[10] when he supported Wayne Goss's Labor Government closure of inefficient rail workshops in his own electorate of Ipswich.

A number of determined and capable leaders were also coming up through the QR ranks and trying to confront inefficiency head-on. For example, Glen Mullins (who, in 2014, retired from the company after more than forty years of service) oversaw a major restructure of track maintenance gangs in the 1990s. In reducing the maintenance workforce by thousands, Mullins took his case directly to the front line, going toe-to-toe with many people he had known personally for decades.

While some internal reform was permitted by the government, it also gave the QR board a mandate to expand beyond Queensland. From the early 2000s, the government approved significant investments to enable QR to take on its private competition in the Hunter Valley coalfields in New South Wales and in the rail haulage of container freight between Australian capital cities. As part of this push, the government funded QR's acquisition of NSW-based rail group Interail[11] in 2002 and Melbourne-based food, polymer and plastic transporter CRT[12] in 2005.

Most significantly, in February 2006, QR acquired the train operations business of the Australian Railroad Group,[13] a major grain and iron ore hauler based in the country's biggest grain market of Western Australia.

Leon Allen, the then Queensland head of Institutional Banking and Markets with the Commonwealth Bank of Australia (CBA), and a key advisor to QR in both government and private ownership, sees this as a critical milestone.

'Our view in terms of QR's national ambitions was that you needed to get big or get out,' Allen says. 'They took that advice, and you have to give premier Beattie and treasurer Bligh credit for signing off on a policy that had QR spending $480 million in Western Australia.'

On 1 July 2006, the Queensland Government made its most provocative move yet, when it appointed John Prescott as chair of QR. Prescott does not know exactly why he was approached, but suspects that his previous attempts to reform coal freight rates were a factor.

'The reason I took the job on was that I thought the relationship between BHP, the other miners and the government on freight rates was fractured,' Prescott says. 'And I thought well I'm being asked to do a public duty here, maybe we should try to fix it. I was more concerned with the relationship, than who was right and wrong – it needed to be fixed. I thought that was in Queensland's interest.'

Early on, Prescott could see there was a leadership gap that would need to be addressed in several stages over time. Both the board and the management team needed new capability. The changes to the management team, however, could not happen overnight. As a government business, QR could not pay market rates, restricting its quest for leaders between 2006 and 2008. Even so, it still managed to attract some real talent in this period.

QR would also need different leaders at different times. In 2006 and 2007, Prescott saw that QR had to build the team to do better than it was currently doing. In 2009 and 2010, the company had to further build the team to take on the float. After the float in 2010, the management team would need further change so that the company could become world class.

'Three waves, three stages,' says Prescott.

Shortly after taking on the position, Prescott sought further clarity from Premier Beattie on his intentions. Beattie told Prescott that above all, he wanted the company to be a competitive supplier of rail-based transport services to the people of Queensland and Australia. The premier also made it clear that he would allow QR to go beyond rail where sensible, and that he would be happy with continued growth outside of Queensland, at least to some extent.

The focus on competitiveness suited Prescott, who believed that genuine competition was good for QR.

'The old approach was to retain the market at all costs,' Prescott says. 'But my view from day one was that there was no point in trying to preserve a monopoly position.'

'In fact, the company would have to get better if it was exposed to competition. That of itself would be a useful driver.'

It didn't take Prescott long to realise that QR was missing many of the basics that private sector companies took for granted. There was no focus on the customer, and worse, safety was not the priority it had to be.

'This caused me a great deal of concern because safety simply had to be there from both a moral and operational point of view,' Prescott says. 'There was a lot to do, much more than I had been led to believe.'

Prescott was shocked by the lack of the most fundamental information about customers. He would ask managers for the cost of moving coal for a customer from point A to point B, but all they could tell him was the average cost of moving a tonne of coal in Queensland.

'They couldn't break it up, on routes, or for customers,' Prescott says. 'So you divided 180 million tonnes by some aggregate figure, and it cost x dollars a tonne, didn't it? Mind-blowing stuff.'

Deb O'Toole was also confronted by these commercial demons when she signed on as QR chief financial officer (CFO) in late 2007. O'Toole brought a cyclone into QR but she too found herself surprised by the extent of the challenge.

O'Toole noticed a deep-seated view that because QR was an arm of government, it therefore had a higher purpose. People in all parts of the company would sing a common refrain – 'I don't need to be commercial.'

'For example, our corporate and shared services functions operated like a slop bucket,' O'Toole says. 'There was no accountability and the central guys just did what they liked, and the businesses didn't care because it didn't matter to them what happened. So they would fire all this slop into a bucket during the year, buying stuff and doing stuff. At the end of the year they would slop it out in bowls around the organisation, evenly or unevenly, it didn't matter.'

O'Toole started from scratch with the finance function. Again, the basics were missing. Financial reports were often three months late, there was no cash reporting and capital spending was not clearly tracked.

'Large contracts would come up through the organisation to be signed off and when you asked what the process was which arrived at the recommendations, the answer would be 'oh well, this is just the next project.' Things had to change,' O'Toole says.

Customer relationships were the Achilles heel for the old QR. From the hundreds of small and medium-sized customers that used QR's regional freight service, to the large mining companies that supplied coal, the pattern was set. Despite best intentions, a lack of commerciality, interference from government, and the sense of 'higher purpose' led to widespread dissatisfaction among QR's clientele. Most of the stories of frustration were held quietly behind closed doors. Occasionally, they spilled out into the public domain in horrific technicolour.

The inefficiency in QR's regional freight business famously attracted national media coverage in the early 2000s. At the time, QR was transporting pigs by rail to abattoirs throughout the State. Rather than just simply exiting this loss-making business (which would be politically unpalatable), QR had tried to send a market signal by progressively increasing prices.

Mark Hairsine, a key member of the communications team at QR at that time, and now Aurizon's External Affairs Manager, recalls that some wag calculated that it would have been cheaper for QR to hire limousines for each individual pig. The television current affairs program *A Current Affair* then took the story to a gorgeous theatrical extreme – dressing a pig, known as Boris, to the nines, inserting him in a limo, and filming him as he cruised around Brisbane.

QR's relationships with coal customers were never given the Boris treatment. But by 2007, a year after Prescott became QR chair, they reached breaking point. The core of the tension was the long-term haulage contracts that coal customers had signed with QR. When coal prices dropped in the 1990s, customers fought for contracts that prioritised cost over flexibility. When the boom times returned in the mid-2000s, customers then of course wanted the flexibility they had previously negotiated away.

By 2007, QR found itself in a highly publicised contractual straitjacket. Customers demanded increased haulage so they could take advantage of higher prices, yet the extra capacity simply could not be delivered because their requests had not been made early enough. The lead times for new locomotives, for example, were several years.

This did not stop the customers, however, from bringing matters to a head. Following a path ironically forged earlier by John Prescott and other industry leaders, the mining companies took the argument directly to the politicians, claiming that QR's rail bottleneck was destroying economic value for both the companies and through lower royalties, the government itself.

Under considerable industry and media pressure, the Queensland Government felt compelled to act. In 2007, in concert with the peak body of the mining industry, the Queensland Resources Council, it appointed Stephen O'Donnell,[14] the former CEO of QR's main competitor Pacific National (now part of Asciano), to conduct an independent review of the Central Queensland Coal Chain. The review identified lost coal sales from July 2006 to May 2007 of approximately $900 million, with an additional $300 million in demurrage charges. Rail in general, and QR in particular, was identified as the chief bottleneck.

In his final report in July 2007, O'Donnell recommended that:

- central coordinator be created to oversee the Goonyella supply chain, the largest coal system in Queensland;
- business improvement program be implemented across the chain, starting with rail; and
- QR invest urgently in new rollingstock to carry expansion tonnes.

In the eye of the storm, and with the government urging full implementation of the review recommendations, QR accepted all of the O'Donnell recommendations and announced its plan to order 500 new wagons, 40 new locomotives and investment in a third unloading track for Dalrymple Bay Coal Terminal.[15]

The whole episode underlined how an earnest but unsophisticated commercial approach from a government-owned corporation could deliver perverse outcomes. Operationally and technically, QR was regarded as strong and capable, but a lack of strategic alignment with customers resulted in counter-productive contracts, leading to a volume crisis, erosion of customer relationships, political interference, and then significant capital expenditure.

It lent greater urgency to the plans of John Prescott and the QR board for the next phase of QR reform.

'We knew we had to fix safety, fix the business, focus better on the customer and alter the organisational structure,' Prescott recalls. 'And we had to find someone to drive those things from the top.'

Somewhat surprisingly, Prescott didn't immediately think of Lance Hockridge, despite their considerable shared experience.

'I set my objectives for an executive search firm and they came back with a few people, including Lance,' he says. 'Even then I didn't really focus on Lance because I thought he had a pretty good job and it would be very difficult to attract him.'

· · · · · · · · · · · ·

To an outsider like Hockridge in 2007, the potential attraction of the QR CEO position was not immediately apparent. The company was a sprawling, creaking, complex presence across Queensland, with some tentacles in other States. It was by far the largest rail organisation in Australia, employing more than 15,000 people, and did it all, from carrying peak hour passengers to wagons and containers of freight. There was excessive government interference, and managers and the CEO were left in no doubt that the prime purpose of the organisation was to keep passengers happy on the Brisbane metropolitan rail network. There was a whole generation of work to do to make the company more efficient.

But a jewel lurked amid the inefficiency, a staple of the Chinese and Indian economic miracles. QR's network carried half of the world's traded metallurgical coal, a fact that would continually dumbfound investors who would eventually run their rulers over the QR National IPO documents. It also had a strong thermal coal business, and a foothold in iron ore in Western Australia. Above all, it was an organisation with a rich vein of technical excellence, with teams that were steeped in railroading problem-solving ability and could always be relied upon, particularly in a crisis.

As Hockridge looked further into QR, he could see that, managed correctly, this could be one of the world's great transport companies.

'At Bluescope in Dallas, I had a really challenging role, and was surrounded by great people, and a stimulating community,' Hockridge says. 'But I really began to see the opportunity at QR. The quality of the assets, the strategic position, the people – it was overwhelming. What this business would be capable of, properly managed and led – that was what would get me out of bed in the morning.'

············

The November 2007 appointment of Lance Hockridge as QR CEO was a bombshell, inside and outside the organisation. He was the first-ever QR CEO with a private sector background. He was seen as having a clear change agenda and a charter to transform the commerciality of the business. Although he had managed BHP site closures with considerable sensitivity, stories appeared immediately about his 'toe-cutting' background.

Dave McMah, a thirty-year veteran of QR with strong connection to the company's operating sites in Queensland, says that in the field there was no doubt what the appointment would ultimately mean.

'People were very clear about this,' McMah says. 'They thought it would be a waste of time to bring in John Prescott and Lance Hockridge and not privatise QR in some shape or form. They didn't know when that would be, they didn't know what it would ultimately look like, but they knew that it was going to be something along those lines. And those who hadn't thought about it were very definitely told by the unions that's exactly what was going on.'

John Prescott recalls conversations with government in those years that canvassed partnerships, but never privatisations. Prescott's understanding was that privatisation was off-limits, and he therefore did not see that as the place to start an argument. He did, however, see a need to fast-track a more commercial approach in the company and encouraged management to pursue potential joint venture partners for QR's regional and general freight businesses. Prescott was surprised that when hearing of these plans, the then treasurer, Anna Bligh,[16] asked if QR should use the same model for coal. At that stage, a possible coal partner had not been identified, so this intriguing idea never progressed.

'We realised that we would have to fix the coal business ourselves,' Prescott says.

CHAPTER THREE

Reform and scandal

L ance Hockridge flew in from North America in the first week of November 2007 to begin his life as QR CEO and was determined to make his mark early. Only a month later, catastrophe struck. On 7 December 2007, two QR track maintenance workers, Gary Watkins and Jamie Adams, were tragically killed when they were hit by a track machine at Mindi in Central Queensland. It shook Hockridge to the core, as did another double fatality nearly a year later, in which QR train drivers Rick Weatherall and Michael Smithers were killed in a level-crossing collision with a truck at Cardwell in North Queensland.

Safety had been a mantra at BHP and Bluescope, and Hockridge saw no greater priority at QR. He was absolutely determined to turn the company's safety performance around, and had been given that clear brief from Prescott and the QR board.

'Safety is important because it's hard, it's emblematic, and it's representative of the values and business ethics of an organisation,' Hockridge says. 'Nothing in any field of business endeavour is worth doing at the expense of hurting people. All injuries can be prevented and that's either an article of belief or it's not. If it is, then the rest follows.'

It is, of course, a tired, old commercial cliché that people are a company's greatest asset. But anyone spending any time within QR National/Aurizon will quickly realise that the concern for health and safety of every individual is palpable. Dave McMah knew there was a different approach the moment he met Hockridge.

'Unlike religion, unlike politics, there is not a debate,' McMah says. 'It is a fundamental human right that no one gets hurt at work and every part of Lance's body oozes that out. I remember being out at Banyo (a suburb in northern Brisbane), at a time when an employee had been killed riding home on his motorbike. To see the level of distress that it caused him it might as well have been one of his close family members that had died on that bike.'

Within weeks of Hockridge's appointment, QR launched a major company-wide overhaul of safety systems, function by function, team by team. Hockridge brought in global safety experts Du Pont to design and drive a formal safety improvement program.

In parallel with these efforts on safety, Hockridge turned his attention to leadership. In his first 18 months, there was a complete change-out in management ranks. Six of eight leaders who now reported directly to Hockridge were from external commercial backgrounds. Sixty of QR's top eighty managers were new, external appointments. Hockridge started recalibrating customer relationships, pushed for managers to get full value from workplace agreements, and got on with business reforms, instead of seeking government permission for every move.

The management team that would guide the most tumultuous period in the company's history was diverse and capable. CFO O'Toole, as we have seen, had hit the ground running, building systems from scratch and challenging others to think commercially. Hockridge expanded the responsibilities of Ken Lewsey,[17] a no-nonsense former Brambles executive who had already forced reform of the QR freight business in Western Australia. Lewsey took on the difficult task of building the company's fledging iron ore business into a large scale, commercial operation, as well as achieving profitability for the national container freight business.

Hockridge achieved a coup in luring the successful Pacific National (PN) executive Marcus McAuliffe into QR ranks. A graduate of the elite military academy at Duntroon, McAuliffe had been the driving force behind the successful Pacific National Queensland operation that had taken on all of the Toll Queensland general freight haulage. It was PN's first foray into Queensland and gave QR's competitor invaluable local knowledge and narrow gauge experience, which would be crucial to their subsequent coal contract success in the Sunshine State.

McAuliffe began life at QR being groomed to lead the troubled Queensland regional freight business, but it was clear to both he and Hockridge that he could fix a bigger fish – the QR coal operation. McAuliffe was to make some mistakes along the way, but he oversaw a dramatic turnaround in performance and customer credibility.

Hockridge looked to his old stable to find an assured pair of hands to manage the myriad of people issues within the company. John Stephens was Vice President of Human Resources at BHP Mitsubishi Alliance (BMA) and brought a global perspective, having worked in Australia, Indonesia and Canada.

Two key appointments were designed to jump-start the massive exercise of effecting change on the ground. Lindsay Cooper, a mainstay of QR's operations world for thirty years, was a powerful role model within the organisation. Cooper had started as a trade apprentice, before working his way into supervisor and management positions, and ultimately secured the crucial job as executive general manager in charge of the thousands of employees who worked in QR's mechanical workshops, as well as the teams who maintained QR's extensive and complicated track network. In the first wave of reform under Hockridge, Cooper was appointed to a new position leading operational excellence, with a mandate to break down QR's business silos, pull out unnecessary costs, and drive efficiency in the use of assets.

Greg Pringle[18] grasped the nettle as the leader of corporate services, an arm that provided legal, auditing, environment and safety services to the company.

The calm and methodical former magistrate would lead a mini-revolution in this part of the company.

Pringle examined each function in turn, asking if the company needed it at all. If the function was critical, Pringle's team identified exactly what that area needed to do, how many people were required to deliver that, and benchmarked QR against similar companies. Pringle pegged each function at the lower end of the benchmarked spectrum and said, 'Here's our objective.'

Then came the hardest part. The selection of which people to keep and develop and the identification of those who were not required.

'The initial response from our own organisation was 'you don't understand, we've given these people the tools to dig themselves in, there's nothing we can do",' Pringle recalls. 'I said, "You're right, I don't understand, but what I do understand is that the status quo is unacceptable and the only way we can change this is through the people".'

Pringle's corporate services group reduced its numbers from 147 to 46, while providing a superior service, and taking on two additional disciplines.

Martin Moore[19] was given the somewhat poisoned chalice of managing change in a number of bloated head office functions. QR at the time had several hundred people managing information technology systems, procurement, property and learning and development. Later, as O'Toole moved into a full-time role in the company's privatisation battle, Moore took on all of the traditional CFO functions.

Hockridge plumped for stability and expert knowledge in the Network business, retaining the seasoned Mike Carter as executive general manager, Network. While Carter was a long-standing QR employee, he had international experience as well, having worked for several years with London Underground. Carter had a unique combination of technical knowledge and stakeholder nous, and boasted by far the best senior customer contacts in the company. Respected enormously by Network employees, Carter had built a business that was known for its project management ability, although it still had some way to go in thinking commercially.

Former Ansett and Flight Centre executive, Paul Scurrah, was confirmed in the executive general manager, Passenger role. Scurrah would continue the strong customer-service push in the politically charged part of QR that moved hundreds of thousands of commuters and other passengers around QR's metropolitan network in South East Queensland.

Steve Cantwell, who had acted as CEO while Bob Scheuber was on long service leave in early 2007, was appointed chief operating officer. However, it was clear that there would not be room for two bosses at QR, and before long, Cantwell had left QR. He is now head of the rail business for leading equipment supplier Bradken.

············

The new executive leadership team and their direct reports were a good combination, but Hockridge regrets that a number of highly capable people slipped through the net because of the glacial speed of government approvals. Appointments were taking up to twelve months to confirm. On several occasions, deals were done, individuals were ready to start, but the final sign-off from the minister would take three months.

'Good people just don't hang around for that period of time,' Hockridge says. 'Especially when they were coming to QR because of the challenge not the compensation.'

The wheels of state became such an obstacle to the appointment process that Prescott and Hockridge sought an urgent meeting with premier Bligh and Treasurer Fraser.

'We had prepared a whole raft of examples of this kind,' Hockridge says. 'John said, "We've ticked all the boxes around your process. If you want us to run a company like this, and you're not prepared to give us the authority to do this ourselves, at least don't have things hung up in mindless bureaucracy for months".'

'To her credit, the Premier had that solved pretty much overnight. I figured it was a quiet word to Mike Kaiser, her chief of staff. I've got no doubt that there was a message transmitted to a number of department and agency heads about the Premier's wishes. We noticed an immediate difference.'

With the best team he could muster in place, Hockridge began the process of commercial reform. QR was starting from a long way back. It was demonstrably less efficient than its major competitor Pacific National (PN). Less bureaucratic, with more advantageous workplace agreements and a hard-nosed commercial approach, PN was understandably and deservedly building market share in coal in Queensland. The O'Donnell review, and its focus on QR's deficiencies, enabled PN to present itself as an energetic, customer-focussed new entrant.

••••••••••••

But just as Hockridge was starting to gain some traction on the commercial and customer issues, QR was hit by a series of public scandals that would severely try the patience of the government, and it must be said, QR's embattled CEO.

O'Toole recalls an intensive campaign by *The Courier Mail* (the local Queensland daily newspaper) against the Bligh government, focussing on rail transport performance. Day after day, Hockridge, O'Toole, corporate affairs manager, Mark Hairsine, and the head of the passenger business, Paul Scurrah, would find themselves in crisis mode, strategising about how to deal with the latest issue.

'Almost every day there was a series of questions from *The Courier Mail* that were impossible to answer without personal exposure or political exposure,' O'Toole says. 'It was a nightmare.'

Following in quick succession, QR was at the heart of the 'Gravy Train, Gravy Plane', and Riverfire affairs.

In March 2008, the Labor Party's transport committee asked for a special train to be organised for them to view parts of the passenger network in Brisbane. In an extraordinary act of largesse, QR laid on sandwiches and fruit juice. The outrage was all-consuming. The group was accused of 'secretly commandeering' a QR train, and there were calls for a Crime and Misconduct Commission investigation into the links between QR and the Labor Party.

In April 2008, Hockridge and Prescott organised an information tour for media and analysts of some of QR's key sites. It was designed to signal to the financial markets and customers a new, transparent and commercial approach by the company. The trouble was that a private plane was hired to do the honours – domestic flights would have turned a two-day tour into one lasting four days, making it impossible for many analysts to attend. *The Courier Mail* reported that 'Queensland Rail executives hired a luxury jet from one of the

State's richest men for a first-class tour of company facilities,' while by contrast 'commuters are forced to pack into CityTrain services that regularly arrive late.'[20]

Quickly and painfully, Hockridge was learning about the extreme differences between a normal company and a government-owned corporation (GOC).

'As a commercial enterprise, what on earth was objectionable about taking journalists and analysts to show them the power and capability of this business?,' he says. 'To start dispelling the sense of bureaucracy and lack of customer focus? But in a GOC sense, hindsight would say that was pretty naïve on my part.'

The biggest scandal was Riverfire, an annual government-sponsored community event held at water's edge along the Brisbane River, that culminates in a spectacular firework display and fighter jet fly-by. It had also become a popular corporate hospitality opportunity, in which QR had participated for several years. QR chose to invite its largest customers to the August 2008 event, and the riverside restaurant, Sienna, was booked for the occasion.

Again *The Courier Mail* couldn't believe its luck. Readers were treated to line-by-line descriptions of the lavish fare to be served. The Liberal-National Party Opposition joined the fray, because this was another gilt-edged opportunity to attack the government for misplaced priorities. Again, people spoke of commuters squirming in packed trains while the QR elite dined in splendour at the taxpayers' expense.

Hockridge faced up to his critics and went on morning talkback radio to argue his case. He argued that the dinner, at a total cost of $30,000, was designed as a thank-you to customers that were contributing more than $3 million revenue a day to QR, and indirectly the Queensland taxpayer. QR was engaged in a process with these customers to substantially grow this revenue beyond $3 million a day. While many who listened to the broadcast could not fault Hockridge's logic, the momentum was clearly against QR and public outrage needed to be satiated.

Hockridge, amazed and disappointed by the reaction, cancelled the event. Ironically, taxpayers were still left with the $30,000 bill because the restaurant's policy still required a full payment for a late cancellation. It was a disaster for QR's customer relations – at the time of the cancellation, some interstate customers were mid-flight on their way to Brisbane.

In a post-script which made Hockridge immensely popular with his fellow GOC CEOs, Premier Bligh then announced that all GOCs' future entertainment budgets would be capped, and a rigorous new policy would be introduced.

In the heat of the Sienna restaurant scandal, Hockridge and the QR management team probably could only see the negatives in this extraordinary episode. And yet, it was becoming clear to all, including the government, that in appointing Hockridge and Prescott they had unleashed forces that highlighted an unresolvable inconsistency between a commercial QR mandate and public ownership.

Despite Riverfire, QR's reputation for innovative business strategy was changing. The government in particular was noticing a GOC with ambitious ideas and a restless energy – a long way from QR's previous modus operandi.

· · · · · · · · · · · ·

A core challenge was achieving a more commercial workplace agreement with employees. Hockridge, O'Toole, long-time advisor Robin Franklin and experienced QR industrial relations man, James Shepherd, would be the key figures in this process. O'Toole came reluctantly to this working group, having told Hockridge during her job interview 'I'm up for anything, except industrial relations.'

QR was determined to slay as many sacred cows as possible. There were four key targets – the vanilla agreement structure that meant that businesses had no control over their costs, the union right of veto over decision-making, restrictions on the use of contractors, and a 'no forced redundancy' provision in workplace agreements.

In early 2009, Hockridge also took two pivotal non-IR proposals to government. The first was another plan to reform the Queensland regional freight scene. The second, equally ambitious, was the result of detailed negotiations with a prospective financial/operational partner. With then QR treasurer Brendan Gibson, I represented QR in this negotiation, and ended up working full-time for several months on the project.

Although this partnership proposal was seriously considered, it was ultimately rejected by the government. However, the experience had given us up-to-date knowledge on government processes, and a renewed confidence in our ability to quickly turn an innovative concept into a comprehensive business case worthy of government scrutiny.

By early 2009, therefore, the confluence of issues, good and bad, had led Hockridge to a clear conclusion. He believed that nothing short of a major restructure would save the business. There was significant day-to-day interference by government, and every aspect of the organisation was restricted to some degree by the fact of government ownership. The dead hand of government was palpable, and was felt all the way from the operating sites across Australia to the CEO's office in Brisbane.

This was despite the best intentions of Bligh and Fraser, who had given Prescott and Hockridge a relatively free hand and an open set of riding instructions. Hockridge sensed that Bligh and Fraser were genuinely motivated to make the business work, and had demonstrated this by allowing freedoms in recruitment, restructuring, budget authority and general decision-making.

However, it had become clear that government ownership, by its very nature, would always hold back the QR business, because commercial needs would only ever be one consideration when decisions were made. Hockridge saw that with the arrival of competition in QR's Queensland heartland, this had become an irreconcilable problem.

'The biggest issue was that the government owned one competitor and set rules for dealing with the other competitor,' Hockridge says. 'No matter how even-handed as a matter of reality they were, the perception was always going to be that they were doing things to favour their own business.'

Matt Keenan,[21] lead advisor on the QR National initial public offering (IPO) while at Merrill Lynch, says that by this time government ownership of QR was becoming increasingly inappropriate. 'QR was owned, funded and regulated by government, while servicing global multinational coal companies and competing against private sector operators,' Keenan says. 'It was unsustainable.'

The railroad which had been owned by the Queensland Government for one hundred and forty-five years needed a serious makeover.

CHAPTER FOUR

The brothers

The trade unions in Queensland, as we have seen, have enjoyed a remarkable stranglehold on decisions involving QR over the years. They achieved working conditions that were the envy of workforces across the country.

Among these was a blanket company policy of no forced redundancies, irrespective of commercial circumstances. Past QR management had also volunteered an employee right to no forced 'relocations'. This meant that if any part of the expansive QR operation had to be closed, employees could choose to stay in their location, doing no work on full pay. There was nothing the company could do about this.

The dance steps for the QR Enterprise Bargaining Agreements (EBAs) were well known. Management would talk tough about productivity improvement needing to match wage rises, a long exhaustive talkfest would ensue, and the government would then get involved. At the first threat of industrial action, under government direction, management would cave in.

Hockridge and his team hoped that the EBA of 2009 would be different. QR, however, was not ideally placed for a successful negotiation. Despite his experience with industrial relations at BHP, Hockridge was still getting his head around the industrial relations landscape in Queensland. Chief Human Resources Officer Lyn Rowland had left QR, and interviews were underway for her replacement. As we have seen, experienced BMA Human Resources head John Stephens would win this role and join the company in early 2009. But to help in the meantime, Lance called in the very safe pair of hands belonging to industrial relations expert Robin Franklin,[22] who had worked in senior roles at BP Australia, MIM and Thiess.

The positives for QR were that an experienced industrial relations team had devised, and was determined to implement, an ambitious strategy for the agreement negotiations. James Shepherd held the reins.

'At that time, the unions had an enormous amount of power because they were able to use a small muscle to control the whole body,' Shepherd says.

During the previous EBA discussions in 2006, the passenger group train drivers went on strike at a critical point in negotiations.

'The government prevented us from taking action, the strike went on for two weeks, and the city of Brisbane was crippled,' Shepherd says. 'Trying to get into work by bus or car was absolutely horrendous.'

With public patience running low, the bureaucrats and the then Minister for Industrial Relations, Tom Barton, reached an understanding in 2006 with the unions and QR was instructed to 'roll over'.

The passenger drivers achieved a base salary increase of $3,260 a year, and the increase flowed through to all of their other allowances. With only one agreement in place for all of QR's drivers, that increase was then passed on to drivers working in coal, regional freight and general freight.

'Our coal managers woke up the next day and all of a sudden they needed to pay an extra $3,260 to their guys,' Shepherd says. 'So it was impossible for them to manage their own costs.'

It was no surprise, then, that when negotiations for the 2009 agreement began in 2008, one of the key targets for reform was the unwieldy one-size-fits all framework. Shepherd's team took the opportunity to look at the agreement architecture, which had not been touched for 20 years. They found the system in disarray. While the irrelevant agreements sat on a shelf, a layer of custom and practice had evolved to make sure that trains could still run every day.

'All these deals were done – there were memorandums of understanding, local operating procedures, award clauses, agreement clauses, etcetera,' he says. 'If you worked in rollingstock services in Central or North Queensland, you worked under an award, a corporate enterprise agreement and three separate local employment agreements every day of the week, every minute of the day. You literally needed a degree in statutory interpretation to work out what someone working on a Sunday using a screwdriver should get paid.'

QR was helped by a significant change to national workplace arrangements that had been initiated by the conservative Howard Federal Government, and continued by its successor, the Rudd Labor Government. For the first time, companies traditionally captured by State industrial relations regimes, would move instead into the national system. Critically for QR, the new federal law stipulated that employees could only have one agreement applying to them at any one time.

The State Government ran a case to put QR employees back into the state regime, but QR argued against its owners and the unions, and the case was thrown out.

'The situation where we had five agreements applying to one person just could not be sustained because of the law,' Shepherd says.

In all, Shepherd and his team constructed 20 specific standalone agreements for the QR workforce. Critically, they separated the freight and coal train crew agreement from the passenger train crew agreement.

'Sure, a lot of the provisions were similar and the qualifications for being a train driver were still the same,' Shepherd says. 'But what needed to be different were the routes, the allowances, the different working conditions, because there were big differences in the way that these businesses operated.'

The team launched a major engagement exercise with employees, taking the message about the negotiations to twenty one locations in nineteen days. These sessions worked through the detail of the proposed agreements, as well as the language.

'A clause may have previously said, "when an employee works thirty minutes post their cessation time on a normal shift, that employee shall be paid fifty per cent in addendum to their normal hourly rate for that day so worked",' Shepherd says. 'We tossed that out and changed it to "when you work overtime, you get paid one hundred and fifty per cent for the first three hours."'

The proposed new agreements were not just about simplifying the system. The negotiators were also seeking to remove the wide range of veto powers enjoyed by the unions.

'In the past, we would go to change a roster for example, the unions would wait until the eleventh hour, they'd then put in a dispute,' Shepherd says. 'This dispute argued for the status quo, and that required you to go into consultation. You wouldn't agree in consultation, we would then issue a new roster, and give seven days' notice. On the fifth day there would be another dispute, status quo, back into consultation and on it went.'

Unions were so entrenched in QR that they often played a role in basic day-to-day operational decision-making. An employee could go to his or her manager and ask for an interpretation of a rule, or to do something entirely sensible that was a little out of the norm, and find themselves referred to the union. Or corporate human resources may be pulled in to consult with the union on a solution.

Support was shifting away from a framework in which the union always had the final say. And even on the ultimate sacred cow, the rule against forced redundancies and relocations, QR management was making progress. The Queensland Cabinet gave QR the licence to table a proposal that offered workers the option of giving up the right to no forced redundancy in exchange for a one-off bonus of $10,000.

············

It was early in 2008 that the QR Enterprise Bargaining Agreement (EBA) negotiations had commenced. At that time, there was some sour economic news globally, but Australia was still in the middle of a once-in-a-generation mining boom. Many railway employees across QR had already jumped ship to the more lucrative mining industry. To be able to do this with a $10,000 cash bonus would have been attractive to many.

'Out of the twenty individual agreements, I thought that only one section of the workforce would baulk at removing the no forced redundancy provisions,' Shepherd says. 'That was regional freight in Queensland. There had already been talk of reform and cut-backs in this business. But with the sparkies (electricians) and train crew, they were going gang-busters and there was no talk of redundancies.'

Shepherd's view is that QR employees, even those in regional locations, were beginning to understand that change was critical, even on the long-standing redundancy protections.

'I remember one guy calling me a "pirate, offering your bits of silver to buy conditions off us and our kids." I said, "Well, if I'm a pirate, you're a vandal," Shepherd says. "How long are you going to keep on those digs until the whole house of cards comes down? If you were running a service station and you employ four people and you lose half of your customers, what would you do? Would you make two people redundant and then keep two people on for the next 20 years? Or would you keep all four on, and then have to shut up shop in two years and put four out of work?"'

'They didn't like it, but they got it. Of course, we had to put a $10,000 carrot in front of them, but they still got it.'

Yet as negotiations continued deep into 2008, and the economic news became gloomier, the atmosphere changed. Australia escaped the worst of the global recession of 2008/09, but Australian workers refocused on job security as a top priority. For a time the increasing uncertainty actually helped QR's negotiation strategy. The Hockridge message to unions was that they should support the deal on the table before something more severe came out of left field.

In the end, the government blinked, withdrawing its support for the move to strike out the no forced redundancy provision. Hockridge was called to a meeting with the then Deputy Premier, Paul Lucas. As he entered the building, coming out of the same door was the Queensland Secretary of the Rail Tram and Bus Union (RTBU), Owen Doogan.[23]

'In the end, we got rolled on this because we allowed ourselves to be positioned around the lead up to a State ALP conference,' Hockridge says.

James Shepherd took the news badly.

'I got very upset that night because we'd put five years into getting it to this stage,' he says. 'The team had done a lot of work with the government to get it to a stage where we could put a proposal on the table that would take this company forward in a major way. We were negotiating with eight unions, the Transport Department, the Industrial Relations Department, Treasury, and the politicians, and we were so close.'

············

The 2009 EBA delivered some change, but the reality was that QR's industrial relations framework still put it at a competitive disadvantage. When John Stephens officially took up his post, he immediately saw stark differences with the more flexible and productive arrangements enjoyed by mining companies.

'James and the team did a good job, operating with what they had,' Stephens says. 'But I had just come from a round of EBA negotiations with the BHP-Mitsubishi Alliance (BMA) workforce. Comparing the two was like chalk and cheese. The QR agreement was one hundred and twenty pages long and full of prescription, compared to best in class documents that were twenty pages, clear, simple, very enabling and allowing for flexibility. We had a lot of room for improvement.'

Stephens was also struck by the need to fundamentally change the nature of the relationship between the front line workforce and management.

'The way we operated was a long way from best practice and efficiency. And where I saw the very big difference was at the front line supervisor level. In outside industry, those guys were the front line for management. In our organisation, they were instead the top end of the union movement.'

Stephens brought a philosophy to the company that would elevate the role of the front line leader, making them the key enablers of superior performance. Resonating with a strong view also held by Prescott and Hockridge, Stephens' approach also made front line leaders the main communicators with the workforce.

'Being able to manage safety, that's got to be a front line leader's first responsibility,' he says. 'Secondly, they need to have the tools to manage performance, and engage with the workforce to get the best out of people, to get that discretionary effort.'

It took time for QR to get traction in engaging directly with employees. The unions were a hard habit for people to break. However, with each Queensland coal contract lost to QR's competitor Pacific National, life would become a little more uncertain for the workforce.

In reality, there were really only two choices. The company, and all its employees, could choose to ignore reality and tick along, only to find their key business progressively taken away by an effective competitor, and government turning off the funding tap. Alternatively, people could acknowledge the collective threat, and agree to work together in a different way to hold on to existing contracts, and help grow new business.

Just telling employees that they had to change, however, was not enough. They had to be motivated to change because they wanted it too. After the bruising EBA battle in 2009, Hockridge, Stephens and the rest of the team went heavily into listening mode. From Central Queensland, to the Hunter Valley and Western Australia, a core theme emerged.

'It's all expressed in different ways, but when you ask what employees want out of this business, it's about opportunity – not just personal opportunity but opportunity for their kids,' Hockridge says. 'The opportunity for their kids may be an actual job at QRN, or the opportunity for the kids may come because I've got a good secure robust job at QRN and I can afford to give my kids what they need. Like training and education.'

'There aren't too many people saying, "Gee, I wonder how I can sabotage the company today or drive this company ever more toward being uncompetitive and going out of business." Employees wanted the place to succeed, and so did management.'

The new approach to engagement would have the full support of the board. From the time that he was a line manager with BHP Transport, John Prescott had realised that it was pointless to try to impose your own political or industrial relations view on the workforce.

'What you had to do was find a common purpose,' Prescott says. 'That is, you had to get them to do the same things you wanted to do, even though they would do it for different reasons. You didn't have to convince them that your reasons were valid; you just had to find common ground.'

CHAPTER FIVE

A freedom to roam

When Lance Hockridge joined QR in late 2007, I was working as general manager of national policy for the chief operating officer, Steve Cantwell. I had signed on with QR in 2006 after spending three years working for its competitor, Pacific National.

What kind of a CEO would Lance Hockridge be? We knew he was a veteran of the steel industry, and had worked closely with John Prescott, our chair, when they were both in senior ranks at BHP. The industrial sector in Australia had spawned a number of seasoned executives like Hockridge, who were known for their business savvy and ability to engage large workforces to make things happen. But I wondered how he would respond to a quirky introvert like me.

I nearly didn't get the chance to find out. At the time, I was working in the project management office (PMO) on a project to reform QR's regional freight business in Queensland. Our dramatic turnaround proposal would have involved a number of depot closures and staff reductions, and significant community impact. I had devised a community strategy to lessen the impact of these proposed changes. When it was ready, I emailed the plan to our small select group, including one external consultant. However, I made a catastrophic mistake, and accidentally emailed it to a front-line employee with a very similar name.

Within hours, the plan was in the hands of the trade unions and then, the media. Crisis meetings were convened. The Department of Transport and the Minister for Transport, John Mickel, became involved. The night that the story broke, I agonised over my future and talked things over in detail with my wife Suzy, who has always been the most remarkable support for me. I decided that I would resign, but before doing so I would devise an action plan to help QR deal with the problem I had created.

It was a Saturday morning, and I was in Steve Cantwell's office, bleary-eyed, with two documents – my resignation letter, and my action plan. He immediately tore up my resignation letter and said, 'We don't shoot people in the head for doing their jobs.' The focus then was on what we could do to improve the situation.

Not long after this episode, and just three weeks after Hockridge had started as CEO, Cantwell helped me secure a meeting with the new boss. In the background, and well beyond my official scope, I had been working on an idea for a new QR business. I had fifteen minutes to make my pitch, complete with advertising storyboards and a theatrical presentation. It seemed to be going pretty well, so towards the end of my monologue I over-reached, implying that Hockridge and I needed to get on international flights almost immediately to secure the opportunity I had outlined.

He paused for a few seconds. 'Let me make one or two observations, Stephen,' he said.

Hockridge pointed out, expertly, a number of fatal flaws in my plan. It was clear that I needed to do a great deal more work on the idea if it was to ever see the light of day. I walked out of the office, shattered, and convinced that I had come across as a naïve fool.

Two weeks later Hockridge asked to see me.

'We've been thinking about your role in the organisation, Stephen, and we don't think there's a box in which you logically fit.' Oh God, time to dust off the CV.

'But we love the way you think, and we want to create a job where you spend all of your time thinking about the future. We want you to disturb, disrupt and challenge myself and the chair [John Prescott] strategically.'

I was subsequently interviewed by Prescott, and then offered a unique opportunity to learn from, and challenge, the most senior figures in Australia's biggest railroad at a crucial time in its history. Prescott warned me, however, about the complexity of the role I was taking on, and the subtlety I would need to succeed.

'Stephen, in this role you will have absolutely no legitimate authority, but you can get it with one phone call,' Prescott told me. 'If you ever make that phone call, however, you will have lost the game.'

•••••••••••

To form a view on the best way to manage this new role, I looked around the world at the way other companies approached disruption and innovation. I was particularly taken with the approach of the global food company Cargill. Unusually for a 150-year-old private company, they backed their creativity and intellect with a courage that was quite breathtaking. Every five years, in almost-Soviet style, Cargill aggressively aims to double its revenue. At the start of the five-year period, management has only identified a small per centage of revenue growth. The remainder is labelled the Innovation Gap, and business units are then asked to address this gap by innovating and creating shared value with their customers. A central innovation function at Cargill provides facilitation for these customer interactions.

During my travels, I ran into some of Hockridge's old acquaintances from Bluescope, who provided a further window on what made the man tick.

One told the story of Hockridge hearing of an oddball inventor who was doing outlandish things with everyday products, including trying to incorporate solar panels into paint.

'Let's go and spend some time with that guy,' Hockridge had said. It was another powerful example of his philosophy of diversity and his belief in the continual search for new angles. Diversity is a feature of all of the management teams that Hockridge has put together. He is a great supporter of getting different personalities to fire off each other, and believes that technical capability and naivety are both important ingredients for success.

'If you look at the management teams at QRN, Port Kembla and Bluescope in North America, it's one of the things I've always tried to do,' Hockridge says. 'I look to build a team of cohesion with respect to values, a team which has the right experience and skills, and also people who think differently. I'm the quintessential analytical type person but my basic predisposition is to have people around me who process things in a different way. You need a breadth of capability where 1+1 equals more than 2, especially in circumstances where there is a large change to be undertaken.'

I had decided that although QR had a very good track record in research and development, it was not an environment that encouraged people to take risks with their thinking. I was on the hunt for a set of tools that could be used in a range of settings to inspire breakthrough innovation. After an extensive search, I tracked down a wonderful methodology used by a Boston-based consultancy, Synecticsworld. We trialled this approach, to great effect, for two of the intractable safety issues facing QR – level crossing safety and trackside safety. With a small innovation team led by former marketing specialist Glen Barber, we would use this innovation approach for several years to generate compelling ideas to address big problems. At the same time, team by team, individual by individual, we started to change language and culture. 'To build on that', 'how to' and 'I wish' are now all part of the company's lexicon.

In addition to this 'bottom-up' innovation work, I became heavily involved in strategic plays, like the detailed negotiations with a prospective financial/operational partner referred to earlier. This project was influenced by a 'what if?' brief I had written for Hockridge in late 2008 on this potential partner and the specific opportunity. I have constructed similar 'what ifs' on scores of ideas over the years in this role. In the above case, it led to a real-life project. On other occasions, it is not uncommon for Hockridge to say 'Stephen, that is the single-most stupid idea I have ever heard. But it makes me think of this, which actually has some merit.'

I cannot think of too many leaders, or companies, that would encourage potentially company-changing ideas from someone who on the face of it has no technical expertise. I am not an engineer. I have not led a big operational team. And although I have been in railroading for close to ten years, I would not consider myself a genuine railroader.

My formal qualifications are a journalism degree and an MBA, which I think help me with a sharpness of thinking, and ability to structure a compelling argument. In my private life, my great love is music – writing, listening and playing. What Prescott and Hockridge have done is given me open licence to bring the creative side of my personality to the office. And perhaps most importantly, I have been given time. Of all the senior executives at QR National/Aurizon, I have by far the most white space in my diary.

· · · · · · · · · · · ·

It was during one of my periods of reflection that I did some detailed work on the privatisation of the iconic, government-owned railroad Canadian National.

I first heard of the Canadian National story in 2007. As we have heard, I was working for a few months in QR's project management office, which had been responsible for the Australian Railroad Group (ARG) acquisition in 2006. One book was compulsory reading in the project management ofice – *The Pig That Flew* by Harry Bruce.[24] The book chronicled the incredibly rapid, revolutionary privatisation of Canadian National Railway in 1995. Defying a chorus of naysayers, the Canadian Transport Minister at the time, Doug Young, had pushed through an IPO of the business in double-quick time. Despite predictions of disaster, the IPO was eight times over-subscribed, and netted the Canadian Government $2.16 billion in proceeds. CN's share price doubled in its first year on the market, and it has since gone on to become the most efficient railroad in North America, with an enterprise value more than twenty five times higher than at the time of privatisation.

If QR was ever to be privatised, the accepted wisdom was that it would be a trade sale of the most commercial business (coal), and that the tracks would be separated from the trains, because of the long-standing policy preferences of Australian governments. There had never been an Australian rail IPO – trade sales had been the mechanism for privatising rail in New South Wales,

Victoria, Western Australia, South Australia and Tasmania. Yet here was the most successful rail privatisation ever, CN, sold via IPO with retention of tracks and trains in the one company (vertical integration). On virtually every measure, the parallels were uncanny. At the time of its privatisation, CN had been in government hands for more than seventy years. It was regarded as a slow-moving, bureaucratic monster, yet had great assets. It was privatised by a left-leaning government to deal with a massive budget black hole.

There were some delicious quotes which could have all applied to QR:

> 'The sad sack national rail outfit that has had more fresh starts than Elizabeth Taylor has had husbands.'

> 'With its myriad management layers, overlapping authority, fuzzy lines of command and regional fiefdoms, its structure was a hangover from an era when railways were militaristic within, and lordly without.'

> 'If it spent too little on renewing physical capital, it was damned for backwardness; if it spent too much, it was damned for extravagance.'

In early 2009, I summarised *The Pig That Flew* in a rollicking five-pager for Hockridge, and gave it to him for a weekend read.

CHAPTER SIX

The Queensland Premier shocks the State

Queensland, along with Western Australia, is a state endowed with extraordinary resource wealth. For many years, all of the economic indicators were travelling in the one positive direction – jobs growth, mining royalties, government surplus, economic growth. The collapse of Lehman Brothers and the unravelling global financial crisis in 2008, however, was to punch a hole in Queensland's critical numbers, and its economic credibility. Then came the biggest indignity of all – the loss of Queensland's cherished AAA credit rating.

'All Australian States have carried AAA ratings and they hang on to them with great pride,' says Matt Keenan, a key Merrill Lynch operative who worked on the QR National privatisation. 'Therefore, if you're the odd one out, it creates all sorts of political sensitivity. Of course, many people overseas couldn't really understand the problem. Quite often we have been told "California is bankrupt – what are you worried about?" But it was still a significant concern for Queensland.'

In February 2009, Bligh called an early election on the back of increasingly bad financial news for the State. The credit rating had been hit, and the state had slid into deficit only two months after predicting a surplus. Unemployment was predicted to hit seven per cent within twelve months.

Because of the worsening financial situation, the 21 March poll was seen as an opportunity for the Liberal National Party Opposition to snatch power after ten years in the electoral wilderness.

In the end, the Premier conducted what has been described as a masterly campaign that drew the Opposition Leader, Lawrence Springborg, into a number of tactical mistakes. Springborg announced new spending plans on a regular basis, while the premier held back, the essence of frugality in tough times. Springborg early on announced a $1 billion public service purge, which the government calculated would cost up to 12,000 jobs. This gave the Premier the high ground on employment, and contrasted with the Bligh 'jobs, jobs, jobs' pledge.

The Premier triumphed so decisively that journalists began to imagine a Bligh dynasty stretching into the long-term future. On 22 March 2009, the day after the election win, *The Sunday Mail's* Darrell Giles wrote: 'Her popularity soared and that will continue – if she sticks to her word and introduces a fresh new Labor, supposedly by the end of this week. She was able to step out of former premier Peter Beattie's shadow yesterday, something she promised last July. It was certainly a big shadow. Now she creates her own.'[25]

Yet within months of this sweet victory, the Premier was regarded as a pariah by the union movement and the community in general. And asset sales, especially of QR, were at the heart of it all.

....

At the end of the previous year, O'Toole had a sense that we had reached a stalemate with government over investment.

'We'd been trying to get sensible negotiation for the Goonyella to Abbot Point Expansion (GAPE) project and we were getting abused everywhere,' O'Toole recalls. 'The Treasurer gave us the instruction, "my balance sheet is no longer available for this sort of infrastructure, you better figure out a way to fund it."'

When the government announced the loss of its credit rating, Hockridge and O'Toole could see an opportunity.

'We put a team together to look at the options for a dramatic restructure of QR,' O'Toole says. 'We could see a way that we could help them get their credit rating back.'

The group really didn't start serious work until the eve of the election, and there were no discussions with government until after that election. The first internal 'Project Peter' workshop, facilitated by McKinsey, was held on 3 March. I was part of the small group brought into this sensitive exercise, probably because we were looking for something a little out of the ordinary to grab the government's attention.

While hopeful, the group was also realistic about the chances of success. John Stephens, who was with the brains trust from the very beginning, knew how difficult the challenge would be.

'To be frank, I thought it was an incredibly long shot, but that it was a possibility,' he says. 'And that kept me, and a number of us, going for a fair while.'

The project team approached the key questions with open minds, and ensured that any preconceived views were challenged. Nothing was left off the table, as the team examined the pros and cons of a range of options for the QR business, including the full privatisation of the freight business. The team examined the value story of the transaction options, the superior outcomes available under private ownership, the practicality of achieving a sales transaction, the arguments for and against vertical integration, and what a transaction would mean for jobs, investment and the government's budget bottom line.

After the election, on 28 April 2009, Hockridge met the treasurer to present our findings. We had concluded that the privatisation of an integrated

QR freight entity offered the best prospect of maximising sale proceeds for the government, as well as setting up the organisation for an effective future. We argued that the sale was doable, and that there were a myriad of possible sources for debt and equity capital. Hockridge told Fraser that a sale process, whether it be trade sale or IPO, would take approximately twelve to eighteen months. This would include the significant exercise of separating the freight business from the government-owned passenger railway.

At the time, Fraser and the team at treasury were deep into a comprehensive review of the State's balance sheet, which had been savaged by the global financial crisis. Despite this, Fraser was determined to continue with a plan to increase spending on infrastructure, to fuel the medium term growth of the economy.

'We made the decision to continue with the building program and that meant that there had to be a balancing entry,' Fraser says. 'No one is going to turn up and just donate a new hospital in regional Queensland.'

Fraser noted that Queensland was almost alone among Australian states in continuing to hold very significant commercial businesses on its balance sheet.

'Queensland had a much bigger exposure in a whole range of business areas that in other States were more appropriately being operated, funded and the risks borne by the private sector,' he says.

At QR, we believed that we had constructed a financially logical argument, and that the government was genuinely intrigued by the options. With hindsight, our presentation was probably overly focussed on financial logic. There was little time spent thinking through the political optics, and we had not illuminated the political lessons from previous failed and successful rail privatisations. The idea of privatisation had been seeded, but we had no control over the structure that would result.

Fraser was certainly interested in the genuinely new angle that Hockridge had presented.

'It wasn't until some time after the election that QR came on to the radar, and it was from QR approaching us, rather than us approaching them,' Fraser says. 'Lance approached me and said "I know you're going through a tough budgetary redesign here, here's something you probably haven't thought of." And the truth is I hadn't. QR always seemed like a bridge too far politically.'

However, the more Fraser thought about it, the more he warmed to the idea of at least a partial sale option for QR.

'QR was always going to be one of the more capital hungry entities on the State's balance sheet,' he says. 'You only have to look at the type of business it is, its breadth, its exposure to demand underpinning its fundamentals. They were going to keep coming back. In order to compete and properly service the customer base, they were going to be looking for huge capital in the medium term. The ability for the private sector to provide that I think was compelling.'

However, we clearly misread his interest as support for the idea of an integrated IPO.

'I wasn't initially attracted to the integrated model,' Fraser says. 'I think it represented a step outside the norm in Australia obviously. And the treasury view was inclined towards separating the tracks from the trains.'

On 2 June 2009, the Premier announced a $15 billion program of asset sales to plug the increasing budget deficit hole.[26] The coal assets of QR were part of the package, along with the Port of Brisbane, Queensland Motorways, Forestry Queensland and the Abbott Point Coal Terminal. QR's coal business was expected to raise more than a third of the total proceeds. The premier also said that QR's non-coal freight services would also be considered for sale.

The reaction of Queenslanders was swift, and outraged. The unmistakable impression, fuelled by the media, was that the Premier had been secretly planning the asset sales, and had deliberately kept this from voters. It was a charge from which Bligh never recovered.

The announcement was a crushing blow to Hockridge and the senior team at QR. While the public message from both Bligh and Fraser left some room for manoeuvre, it was clear to us that as things stood, the QR coal business was set to be emasculated and its pieces sold to separate bidders. There was no clarity for the other freight businesses, which would be 'considered' for sale. And the QR-related transactions were not scheduled until the end of the government's announced three-to-five year time frame for the asset sales. The RTBU was quick to highlight this long lead-time as an opportunity to erode the government's resolve on rail privatisation.

Hockridge was contemplating a future as a lame duck CEO presiding over a dispirited organisation that progressively lost slices of valuable business until it finally stumbled into the private sector in several, uncoordinated bits. The potential to be one of the world's great transport companies would be lost.

'The lead up had been a summons to a meeting with the Treasurer the night before,' Hockridge says. 'There were meetings with much sitting around, and then the treasurer saw us, and it was very much a case of tablets from the mount. There was no hint or suggestion of any consultation around this. He'd simply laid out what was coming.'

Given all the work that had been done, Hockridge was bitterly disappointed.

'I was disappointed about the lack of consultation and the announcement itself. But I wasn't surprised. I think we'd predicted that was the way they would go.'

O'Toole says this was the worst moment for her in the whole privatisation process.

'Lance was dumbstruck, we were dumbstruck,' she says. 'And in my usual fashion I tried to point out to the Treasurer that he shouldn't lock himself into certain things. I also pointed out some strange things – do you really want the ARTC (Australian Rail Track Corporation) taking over Queensland track? But he was too far down the track. He'd just come out of a Cabinet room where he'd been fighting for his political life. It was only through courtesy that he actually spoke to us. We were third cab off the rank, after the unions.'

It was 1 am the next morning and Hockridge and O'Toole were sitting in Hockridge's office, still processing the news they had received.

'We were just so deflated, we couldn't think of anything to do,' O'Toole says. 'It was over. Two years of absolute hell. Absolute hell, it really was.'

At around 2 am, they took a deep breath and rang the chair.

'He was in some African country and the line kept dropping out,' O'Toole says. 'He was great, incredibly supportive. We decided before we resigned we would have the chair go see the Premier. After a lot of thinking we worked out that the outcome we wanted was an ability to go back to her with a better option than the one she had announced.'

In follow up meetings, Bligh and Fraser gave a commitment that they would receive a submission from QR on alternative options. The government had announced that it would finalise its asset sales structures, and timeframes, during a three-month scoping study to be completed by November 2009. This was our chance.

O'Toole says our second effort to convince the government to keep QR together had to be dramatically different.

'We had to start managing the political dimension,' she says. 'In June, we had come up with all the ideas, made the presentations, and given the treasurer the whole package – and he didn't even spend five minutes testing it with us. That's what woke us up. These people don't think like we do. We're speaking Swahili over here.'

CHAPTER SEVEN

Policy battle lines are drawn

Jim Betts, former Victorian Secretary of Transport and now a key figure in Infrastructure NSW, is a cool guy. He refuses to wear a tie, and has a poster of Nick Cave in his office. He is also someone who gets things done.

For the most part, however, transport policy in Australia is traditionally either frustrating or pretty jolly boring. It has become a poster-child for finger-pointing between state and federal governments, and where reform does occur, it does so with the speed of an arthritic snail. It took ninety-four years for Australia to achieve a standard gauge rail link from Perth to Brisbane. And it took nearly ten years for everyone to finally agree on establishing a single national rail safety regulator, instead of seven state and territory bodies.

For real reform to happen, there has to be a powerful politician who sees a need to take action and is unswerving in its execution. It happened when London Mayor Ken Livingstone courageously introduced a congestion charge for the city in 2003. It happened when Australian Prime Minister John Howard decided to toughen the gun laws in the wake of Tasmania's Port Arthur massacre in 1996. And it happened in the 1980s when the British Prime Minister Margaret Thatcher invented a way of making a raft of revolutionary privatisations popular by using them to create a 'capital-owning democracy' in the United Kingdom.

Thatcher started tentatively with refuse collection, but then fearlessly tackled the elephants in the room – including British Telecom, British Gas, Rolls Royce, British Steel, British Airways, and British Petroleum (BP). The 1986 'Tell Sid' television campaign that encouraged Mums and Dads to invest in the float of British Gas underscored the political positives available – providing share prices continued to rise.

After Thatcher had made privatisation fashionable, it became a popular tool for reformist governments across the world. Emerging economies in Africa, Asia and Eastern Europe would use full privatisations or 'concession' government assets to kick-start investment in key industries. Existing champions of the private sector such as Canada and the United States would go further by privatising most of the remaining government businesses, including key railroads like Canadian National and Conrail. And in Australia, state and federal governments would each decade steadily release a handful of government businesses into the private sector. Unlike in the UK or the USA, however, most of these transactions would be trade sales, rather than public floats.

Despite the vote-winning potential of happy shareholders, the core reason for privatisation in most cases was that it made economic sense. The most active privatising government in Australia was the Liberal/National Party Kennett Government in 1990s Victoria. In two terms, Premier Jeff Kennett privatised the State's gas, electricity and transport assets, as well as several prisons. In May 2011, *The Australian* reported that a study by the Energy Users Association of Australia found that the government-owned electricity networks in Queensland and New South Wales were charging prices that were double those charged by private operators in Victoria.[27] Kennett expounded his privatisation philosophy when speaking to the ABC's *World Today* program in 2008 about the need for the privatisation of the supply of electricity: 'The benefit is two-fold,' he said at the time. 'One, you get greater competition in terms of pricing, and that is always good for the consumer. And secondly, you get the opportunity to have the private sector upgrade a lot of what is clearly decaying infrastructure.'[28]

Sir Rod Eddington, former Chair of Infrastructure Australia, says managing limited funding is an ongoing challenge for government.

'There are many calls on government budgets, not only hard infrastructure, but also soft infrastructure like health and education and welfare,' he says. 'But it's very clear that government funding is limited. One of the ways in which a state can give itself the capital it needs is by selling existing assets that are perfectly at home in the private sector.'

'I see the QR float as part of this overall journey. This is a quality asset that has a history of state ownership but naturally sits in the private sector. Selling it means the government has given itself a substantial capital base from which to invest and drive new projects.'

Despite Queensland Governments of all colours earning a reputation as 'agrarian socialists', the Sunshine State has actually not been idle on privatisations. Most recently, the Beattie and Bligh Labor Governments over 10 years had privatised the TAB gaming business, energy retailers, the Cairns and Mackay airports and the Golden Casket Lottery.

But the QR privatisation would be very different, chiefly because of its presence in almost every Queensland community, and the controversy generated by its sale structure. It is this debate and the subsequent decision by government to opt for the most 'courageous' option before it, that sets this privatisation apart from the rest.

············

The genesis of the battle over the structure of QR National was Australia's National Competition Policy (NCP) reforms of the 1990s. At the time, government businesses were put on notice to prevent them misusing monopolistic market power. For existing telecommunications, rail, and ports operators, NCP ushered in a new world of third party access to their infrastructure.

And importantly, the agreement between the States and the Commonwealth would present obligations and conundrums for governments contemplating the sale of any asset that looked or smelled like a monopoly. Under the Competition Principles Agreement (CPA) of 1995, any government considering such a move needed to review 'the merits of separating potentially competitive elements of the public monopoly.'[29]

South Australia, Tasmania, Victoria and Western Australia all privatised their freight railways after this agreement was signed. As required under the CPA, they all considered the separation of tracks from trains. But instructively, after reviewing this option, every one of these States decided to sell their railways as vertically integrated entities.

Each of these transactions was a trade sale to a single buyer. The treasuries that ran these processes took market soundings early on to indicate interest and potential proceeds. And invariably, they found only lukewarm market interest in separated freight railways. Potential buyers simply saw additional risk in a separated structure and a more complicated value proposition. Another factor was that a number of mid-tier North American railroads were involved in offshore acquisitions during this period. Genesee and Wyoming (in joint venture with Wesfarmers) picked up the freight railways in South Australia and Western Australia, and Rail America was successful in bidding for the Victorian freight network. These companies ran vertically integrated railways in their domestic geography, and were not prepared to experiment with new models offshore.

The governments involved in these transactions were also keenly interested in structuring the new companies so that they could operate independently from day one, preferably without any ongoing government subsidy. Vertical integration was considered a structure that was best to give the new owners the required strength and flexibility to make this happen.

Unfortunately, the underlying characteristics of some of the privatised railways, in particular in Victoria and Tasmania, meant that the structure was largely irrelevant to their prospects. Freight railways in Victoria and Tasmania are characterised by short hauls, light and volatile levels of traffic, and low value commodities. This makes their railway businesses extremely vulnerable to competition from trucks, and unforeseen circumstances like drought. Rail privatisations in Victoria and Tasmania ultimately gave way to re-nationalisation when private owners were unable to make them work commercially.

The vertical integration trend in Australian rail privatisations was broken by the process that created Pacific National, now part of the infrastructure company Asciano. The federal government-owned National Rail Corporation, which had been formed out of a collection of loss-making state freight railways, was at the time of the NCP vertically-integrated. It had been corporatised and was being groomed for ultimate sale to the private sector. This included the purchase of an entire new locomotive fleet, known as the NR Class, which is still the main workhorse of the inter-capital city freight rail system.

In the wake of NCP, the Federal Labor Government led by Paul Keating decided to explore options for separating track and train operations for its government-owned railway organisations. The initial reform was the creation of a track access division within Australian National. The government then decided to implement full structural separation, creating a separate entity to own and manage the track. The Australian Rail Track Corporation (ARTC) was established in 1997, and quickly moved to encourage competition between operators. Soon, National Rail found itself competing with the New South Wales (NSW) Government's rail freight arm Freightcorp and Toll Rail on track that it had previously controlled itself. This was early evidence that vertical separation could create an environment for greater competition.

Coincidentally, the NSW Labor Government, with Bob Carr at its helm, was also preparing Freightcorp for sale, and at a key stage, the NSW and Federal Governments decided to combine their processes. As with National Rail, Freightcorp was to be a pure 'above rail' company, with the rail track held separately by government through the Rail Infrastructure Corporation. Unlike the volatility of the businesses underpinning the privatisations in Tasmania and Victoria, this privatisation would have scale and greater stability. The container freight strength of NR and the coal dominance of Freightcorp in the Hunter Valley provided much-needed resilience for the company that would soon be known as Pacific National.

National Rail and Freightcorp were acquired in a trade sale by joint-venture partners Toll and Patrick for $1.2 billion, making it at that stage the largest Australian rail privatisation. Toll was the largest logistics company in Australia, while Patrick owned container ports in each capital city. Although the joint venture was to run into major difficulties in the future, at the time of the transaction it looked a logical combination of assets and philosophies. Toll Rail of course immediately ceased its operations, subsuming them into the new Pacific National operations, which now held a dominant market position in container haulage between capital cities, and in the movement of Hunter Valley coal to the world's largest coal export port in Newcastle.

Meanwhile, in Queensland, there continued to be no sign of rail privatisation or vertical separation. Queensland Rail was, however, corporatised, and a third party access regime established in line with NCP requirements.

The upshot of all of this activity was that Australia had essentially developed two vastly different philosophies for running freight railways. One put a premium on the efficiency interface between tracks and trains, and the strength of a diversified business. The other emphasised the importance of structural separation and 'above rail' competition. That these two schools were never completely reconciled would become dramatically clear as the QR National transaction developed.

CHAPTER EIGHT

Inspiration from abroad

If I ever get to be a contestant on Mastermind, my special subject will be 'Rail Privatisations Across the World.' For close to twelve months, global rail case studies were my life. And I was not alone – QR had a large team dedicated to the task of bringing these dusty old stories to life, particularly their political dimensions.

After Bligh's June 2009 announcement signalled its likely break-up, QR obviously had to find something special to deflect the government from its course. Hockridge convened a group of true believers to direct and drive our battle for survival. I began working full-time on this issue as part of a 'war-room' group that included Hockridge, O'Toole, our relentless Corporate

Affairs Manager, Paul Cronin, John Stephens, Bob Herbert and Dr Terry Cutler. Bob Herbert, a former head of the Australian Industry Group, was well connected politically and industrially. Terry Cutler was on the CSIRO board with O'Toole, and had priceless experience of previous high profile privatisations, including Telstra. There were other crucial players in the core group, none more so than the Network's Mike Carter, who brought to every critical decision a deep knowledge of customers, international structures (given his United Kingdom experience), and rail infrastructure mastery.

The Bligh Government had moved quickly to appoint a Transaction Team, made up of senior Treasury figures and banking advisors. Deputy Under Treasurer, Tim Spencer, would lead the team. An inscrutable, systematic operator, Spencer would become a key relationship for us to manage.

Brendon Gibson, the towering firestorm at the helm of QR's finances, had previously worked in Queensland Treasury, and understood what made the bureaucrats tick. He was appointed to lead the QR analysis work for the scoping study. The team moved into dedicated offices, and with a strong McKinsey team providing analytical and strategic help, set about the Herculean task of assessing all of the options.

It was hard to get traction. Our advice was not particularly welcome, because we were seen as having a vested interest in arguing against the announced model.

We looked not only at the privatisation successes in Canada and the USA (Conrail was a successful Reagan era rail IPO), but also the various failures in Britain, New Zealand and other Australian States. Britain was the most extreme case imaginable – the government of John Major had separated the old British Rail into more than 100 companies between 1994 and 1997. This experiment ended in disaster, with several multiple fatality accidents, and the eventual bankruptcy and re-nationalisation of the privatised track company, RailTrack.

Looking around the world, the overwhelmingly preferred structure for railroads involved keeping both the rail track (commonly referred to as 'below rail') and the operation of the trains and wagons ('above rail') in the same company. This was known as vertical integration.

It was only really in Europe, the UK and Australia the reformers had experimented with separating the ownership of the below and above rail elements of a railroad. In these jurisdictions, there had been a decidedly mixed bag of success. No one, other than the Brits, had tried to simultaneously separate and fully privatise a railroad. Even in parts of the world where policy settings favoured separation, in practice governments had mostly chosen privatisation structures that kept railroads together.

Although the European policy preference for vertical separation was primarily motivated by the need to encourage inter-connectivity between European railroads, there developed also a core belief that a separated structure would promote greater competition between train companies who operated 'above rail' and therefore a superior overall economic benefit. Yet with resource railroads like QR National, there are usually a handful of large, powerful customers who have what is known in the economic trade as 'countervailing power', which describes how one group's market power can balance the power of another group. The dynamics of such a system can provide competitive tension without the need for structural separation.

In an integrated structure with competition between train operators guaranteed by regulation, large mining customers may:

- choose the incumbent
- choose the competitor
- choose a mixture of the two
- run their own trains
- or, in extreme cases, build their own railways.

Building your own railway sounds far-fetched, but it is exactly how the Pilbara was developed, and what a number of organisations have planned to do in Queensland in recent times – including BHP, the Indian power company Adani, the thermal coal joint venture between GVK/Hancock, and the Queensland coal operations planned by Clive Palmer's Mineralogy.

Canadian National continued to beckon us as the most compelling story of privatisation. I used all the public and private sources I could find to gain insights about the personalities involved in the successful privatisation of CN in 1995. Four men were central to the CN achievement – Transport Minister Doug Young, then Finance Minister Paul Martin (subsequently Prime Minister),

CEO Paul Tellier and CFO Michael Sabia. Young was the bull, Martin was the statesman, Tellier was the bridge, and Sabia was the work machine.

Young and Martin were both self-made millionaires, unusual for left-ish politicians, and this business-savvy would help them in making the right calls on privatisation. Tellier was arguably a strange choice as CEO, given that he was a self-confessed 'railway ignoramus', but as the former head of the bureaucracy, he knew how government worked. He surprised many by succeeding in major reforms of CN to help get it ready for privatisation. Sabia made sure that all of the detail was covered, and that the transaction could be delivered at the breakneck speed demanded of decision-makers.

The other key feature of the Canadian National success was that they had done their homework. Tellier and his chair, David McLean, toured the world to look at the best and worst of past privatisations. They spent time in London examining the British Rail experience, as well as the privatisation of British Steel. Doug Young would later say 'If you want to know what not to do, then look at British Rail. It was like the cast of Monty Python had suddenly got their hands on a railroad.'

We realised that our own due diligence tour of real privatisation examples was possible, and desirable. It was late July 2009, and the government had just appointed leading investment banks Rothschild, Merrill Lynch and Royal Bank of Scotland (RBS) as advisors on the asset sale process. We still had a good three months before the scoping study would get to a decision point. It was time to visit the world.

Lance Hockridge and I spent two weeks in Europe and North America in August 2009. With two weeks' notice, we inveigled our way into diaries and boardrooms using every contact we had and every trick in the book. It was summer holiday season in the Northern Hemisphere, so it was amazing that we managed to see whom we did.

Merrill Lynch in Canada were champions – their seasoned Montreal representative Guy Savard opened doors to Young and Martin. My friend Terry Gilliam, from Synecticsworld, used his contacts to help track down Tellier, and also set us up with Matt Rose, CEO of massive US Class 1 freight railroad Burlington Northern Santa Fe (BNSF). QR's international representative, Brian Bock, secured us meetings with a senior manager at the

German government-owned rail company, Deutsche Bahn, and key players at the UIC (an international rail organisation based in Paris).

In the week before we left, O'Toole had established contact with Sabia and spent an hour comparing QR's financial challenges with those that had faced CN. O'Toole opened the door to us meeting Sabia when we were in Montreal, although it would take me five or six conversations with Sabia's personal assistant to finally settle on a time. So as we left Brisbane, we were well positioned, having secured meetings with the top four figures in the CN privatisation – Young, Martin, Tellier and Sabia. Our expectations were high, and we hoped that the Canadians would not disappoint.

This was all to come later. We started our trip badly, in Europe. Over a couple of days in the former seat of world power, we grew increasingly irritated and frustrated by the European approach to business and government. At the time there was a bitter internal power-play taking place within the main global railroad organisation, the Union Internationale des Chemins de fer (UIC) which reminded us of some of the excesses you would expect in the European Union. Old scores were being settled behind the scenes, while on the surface there was civility and interminable discussion. We escaped Paris at the earliest opportunity and hoped for more hard-nosed business interactions in Berlin. We were to be disappointed. Deutsche Bahn (DB) had been pushing for privatisation for more than a decade, but its version of privatisation was from another universe.

The latest proposal, which had been recently iced by Chancellor Angela Merkl, was for DB's infrastructure to remain in public hands, and for twenty-five per cent of its freight train business to be sold to private interests. A sure-fire way of disappointing everyone, including investors, and having no impact on a government railway culture. There was very little for us to learn from the Germans.

•••••••••••

Hockridge and I arrived in Montreal knowing that it was the key. We had read *The Pig that Flew*, but would the actual experience live up to the hype? How compelling was the story when you heard it from the people who had made it happen?

Our biggest day in Montreal had just begun, and I was at breakfast waiting for the boss. Our schedule included meetings that day with Young, Martin and then dinner at Tellier's club. Hockridge sighed as he sat. 'I didn't sleep and I feel like death,' he said. Oh no, not on our biggest day.

During the day, there was not a single sign that Hockridge was not on top form. He played out of his skin. Every meeting was a corker.

We had read about the larger than life Young. He had grown up in an impoverished area of New Brunswick, qualified as a lawyer, and then built himself into a successful businessman. He hadn't forgotten his roots, though, and jumped at the chance to enter politics, on the Left. He quickly gained a reputation as a fixer, someone who could get things done. So unusually for a large financial transaction, the privatisation of Canadian National was left in the hands of the Minister of Transport.

When we first met him in the Merrill Lynch Montreal boardroom, Young leapt towards us, all smiles, and then spoke at ballistic speed for three hours non-stop. You could see why he had been such a formidable politician, but also why he needed to move on after he had spearheaded big change. He would simply have been too exhausted to continue. Young would subsequently become a friend and mentor for Hockridge, the board and the QR National management team, visiting Australia no less than three times during the complicated QR National saga.

Young's messages were clean and unblemished – you need a champion, you need to do it quickly and the transaction must be simple, or the investment market won't support you. It quickly became apparent that Young himself had been the champion for the CN transaction. At a later meeting, Sabia said 'Doug Young was just a bull – the management of CN gets the credit, but Young was the guy. A champion inside the government is so important.' At this stage we were struggling for consistent, courageous political leadership on our issue, but ultimately Queensland treasurer Fraser would emerge as the unequivocal QR National champion.

Young recalls the first meeting with us vividly. He says he was expecting a real tough nut, a more typical railroad CEO.

'When I met Lance, he was the antithesis of someone like Tellier,' Young says. 'Here was this very thoughtful, carefully spoken individual. I immediately wondered if he would have the toughness. I guess you can't judge a book by its cover.'

Martin, former Finance Minister and Prime Minister of Canada, was a commanding presence. Like Young, he was a self-made businessman. Unlike Young, he was a political survivor, who had used the tough decisions as Finance Minister to springboard himself into the top job. We found that Martin had both a memorable turn of phrase and a cut through manner when required. 'You want the company to succeed – the worst thing you can do is constrain it,' he said. 'Make sure it has the assets to succeed. It will become a huge political problem if it doesn't succeed.'

We found ourselves wishing that Premier Bligh and Treasurer Fraser were flies on the wall. And then it dawned on us that we could, and should, orchestrate that. We were essentially conducting job interviews for the credible third party voices who could provide insights to decision makers in Australia. Young and Martin were both hugely impressive, in different ways, and would both actively assist the cause later.

Our Canadian hosts were both dumbfounded by the Queensland Government's proposed transaction timeframe of three to five years. 'Don't mess around – five years is nuts,' Martin said. Young thought it was investment suicide – 'You will scare the hell out of investors. They won't want to put $10 million into kicking the tyres on something as uncertain as this.' We had to move QR National up the batting order.

'If there's anything, anything, that I can do, please let me know.' Both of the ex-politicians recognised the kindred spirit between CN and QR, and were keen to be involved in a second railway miracle.

'Are you the two Australians I have heard so much about?' Tellier, close to seventy, bounded up the stairs of the Mount Royal Club in central Montreal, and ushered us into his private world. After some initial moments of tension, Tellier and Hockridge settled into a vibrant comparison of CEO experiences. Tellier was the perfect host, and gentleman, as waiters in white gloves attended to our every need. During the conversation, Tellier had been incredibly supportive of what we were trying to achieve. He, too, was impressed by the parallels between QR and CN. As a Rio Tinto board member, it must have been awkward for him to be so generous with his time and support.

In the months to come, after Rio and the other miners mounted what was effectively a hostile takeover bid for the QR National track, it would become very awkward indeed.

············

We saw a third Canadian politician before we left Montreal. With very low expectations, I had basically 'cold-called' Ed Lumley, a long-serving director of CN, and a former parliamentary secretary in the Trudeau Liberal Government between 1976 and 1978. Amazingly, he was intrigued by our story, and rescheduled his diary to enable us to meet.

Lumley had been the middle man between Tellier and Young and Martin. Many of his comments hit home. 'The key to getting Caucus support was that this move had nothing to do with railroads, it was about health care. Otherwise, how were you going to pay for the health care people needed?'

Lumley introduced us to a crack financial engineer who worked on the CN deal, Gordon Lackenbauer. 'Gordy' was as sharp about the details in 2009 as he obviously had been in 1995. He had lived and breathed the deal for nine months, including playing the role as the 'under the radar' financial media contact. The ability to background the right journalists at the right time is a critical capability in getting large deals across the line, particularly those with an element of controversy. The QR privatisation team was soon to learn this lesson the hard way. Lackenbauer expounded a principle underpinning the CN deal that would ultimately be central to the QR National transaction.

'The principle on the financial structure was that the company had to be investment grade,' Lackenbauer said. 'Later we were able to do the analysis, and come to a specific conclusion that the rating agencies were comfortable with, but the key was to establish this principle up-front.'

We were struck by the umbilical connection between the financial and political messages – set the company up for success, make sure it is investment grade.

············

From Canada it was a quick pit-stop in Dallas, where we spent a memorable day being entertained by Matt Rose and the management team at BNSF.

This was just months before Warren Buffet, widely considered the world's most successful living investor, paid $42 billion to buy control of BNSF in a momentous vote of confidence in the future of North American freight railroading. Our team saw it as one of the most powerful investor votes of confidence in the vertically integrated railroad model.

The night before we set off back to Australia, Hockridge received a text message that angered and disappointed him. Premier Bligh had just announced to parliament that all of the non-coal track would be retained by the government, and would not be part of the QR National privatisation. Hockridge had been led to believe that he would be consulted on any major moves of this kind. It was not a good sign. Sitting in his former home city of Dallas, half a world from where key decisions about QR were being made, Hockridge wondered again if the struggle was going to be worth it in the end.

CHAPTER NINE

The policy battle

On returning to Australia, Hockridge was confronted by a definite frosty undertone in QR's dealings with government. The government had made its announcement, a trade sale and separation, and many thought the die was essentially cast. Policy experts in Treasury were cradling the Competition Principles Agreement in their arms. The mining industry was celebrating a 'sensible' government decision. Employees were resigned to a split between coal and the rest of the business.

Our team's road back would depend on strong government relationships, and yet our links were cooling, typified by the lack of consultation on the regional track decision. Before we could hope to bring the Canadian example to life, we needed to shake the foundations of the seemingly immoveable Government 'policy' of vertical separation. As we have seen, Treasurer Andrew Fraser saw no reason to doubt the strong advice coming from his Department.

This issue was key to our success or failure, and yet in August 2009 we were very poorly positioned. We had no central National Policy function drawing on analysis from regulatory experts (happily, this has since been corrected in Aurizon). As a former public affairs operative, I had a working knowledge of the issues and some of the players, but my networks were limited. The diversity of our brains trust came to the rescue.

Terry Cutler, veteran of numerous regulatory adventures including those affecting Australia's biggest telecom Telstra, knew Allan Fels, the former boss of Australia's anti-trust watchdog, the Australian Competition and Consumer Commission (ACCC). Cutler suggested we commission Fels to provide an objective assessment of the structural options for the QR privatisation.

I had grown up hearing Fels' unusual voice on multiple competition issues in the 80s and 90s. He was highly respected, and still carried enormous weight in business and government circles. Cutler contacted him to gauge his interest and availability. It would be possible, but the timeframes were tight, which suited us. I then agreed a scope of work with Fels in August 2009, and he and his impressive assistant Sam McSkimming compiled a comprehensive assessment of the issues facing the policy-makers in Queensland.

Fels concluded: 'Railroads are not analogous to electricity lines, gas pipelines or telecommunications networks where access has undoubtedly promoted competition. Unlike in these sectors, railroads require a very intimate and ongoing coordination of infrastructure and the services provided by that infrastructure.'[30]

And further: 'Structural separation is a costly remedy with the potential to undermine the efficient day to day operation of a rail network, as well as reduce the timeliness and cost-effectiveness of investment. It is a remedy which has rarely been applied and is arguably not worth pursuing.'

It was an extremely important and persuasive piece of work, which a number of us worked through in detail, absorbing its critical insights. Expectantly, in September 2009, we shared the document with the Treasury sale team, and the Treasurer himself.

While their reaction was polite, we understood that Treasury remained unconvinced. Fels and McSkimming were told in follow up discussions that the Government's 'policy' was still separation. This was despite the fact that the CPA only required a government to review the option of separation when privatising. This is what the governments of Western Australia, Victoria, Tasmania and South Australia had done before deciding on vertical integration.

It became apparent also that the Fels paper was regarded as a general exposition of structural issues in rail, rather than a work that zeroed in on the challenges facing policy makers in Queensland. It is true that the paper referred regularly to intermodal rail, which arguably has very different economic characteristics to rail coal haulage. Would the conclusions apply equally to the Queensland coalfields? In what way would integration really facilitate timely and efficient investment in the coal network? While vertical integration may be a good idea for lightly trafficked general freight and grain lines, the argument ran, you need full structural separation to create real competition on high volume resource lines.

Our team was hearing similar questions from senior federal bureaucrats, who had heard promises before from companies buying railways. An often-quoted case study was Victoria. The integrated Victorian freight network was bought by Rail America in 1999, who then sold it to Pacific National in 2004. Both transactions brought high hopes for renewal and expansion. Yet ultimately, after years of drought, and little investment, the network ended up back in the hands of the Victorian Government in 2007.

In response to these various misgivings, in mid September 2009 I commissioned Fels to complete a follow up study focusing on Queensland coal.

Sam McSkimming spent several days talking to senior managers and technical experts at QR to understand the complexities of our different coal systems, the development of competition, features of contracts, and the nature of our key coal customers. Fels and McSkimming again hit a tough deadline and this report was available well in advance of the scoping study conclusion.

This report began to get real traction. For the first time it delved into the significant 'countervailing' power of the coal customers, who in many cases were many times larger than QR National would ever be. It was also the first time that the prospect of mining companies owning the track had been seriously explored. Months before the coal companies, led by their representative former Liberal New South Wales Premier Nick Greiner, announced a counter bid for the QR National track, Fels said:

'Common ownership between track and mine may create a new competition problem. An arrangement that integrates coal mines and haulage services may, depending on the model, amount to an anti-competitive agreement. It would depend on the prospect of such an arrangement allowing coal mines to exclude rivals, or raise rival's costs, or otherwise substantially lessen competition in the coal market.'[31]

This report was delivered to Treasury in October 2009. In addition to this depth of analysis on the issue of vertical integration, we were also heavily engaged on financial and operational questions with Treasury and its advisors. At one point, QR National senior executives and operational leaders, including Mike Carter and Deb O'Toole, spent five consecutive days with the scoping study advisors.

During October and November, we dispatched scores of reports in response to myriad questions from the study advisors. Inevitably we would come back to the question of vertical integration. Towards the end of the process, we were given 12 hours to come up with a 20-page summary of the impact of vertical separation on meeting the government's seven specified sale criteria.[32] With McKinsey's help, we crystallised the arguments once more and pressed send.

············

The arguments were one thing. Political insight was quite another, and we always knew that this would be impossible to put on a page. So we had been working for several months on a program of interactions that would make the politics of rail privatisation real for the Premier, the Treasurer and the Transport Minister. One of our first moves had been to invite Doug Young out to Australia to see Treasurer Fraser and compare privatisation experiences.

Young is a North American, but has an encyclopedic knowledge of Australia, courtesy of his previous experience as a board member of the Australian Railroad Group in Western Australia. His knowledge of Australian mining companies, therefore, is informed by twin experiences – in Australia and in North America. I greeted Young at the Stamford Plaza hotel in Brisbane's

CBD just two hours after his 20-hour flight from Montreal had touched down in Brisbane. With flowing grey locks and a ruddy complexion, he looked like a Hollywood leading man, and was clearly champing at the bit. 'I don't seem to suffer jet lag and I can sleep anywhere and anytime,' he said. He was able to take this freshness into meetings from the word go.

Young was a phenomenon, able to effortlessly mix political insight with good business sense. He had long discussions with both Treasurer Fraser and the Transport Minister Rachel Nolan and was able to communicate the epoch-making nature of Queensland's opportunity. Young also held a series of meetings with directors of the then QR Limited, and encouraged them to play a more active role in the campaign for an integrated IPO. Ultimately, the new directors of QR National would display an extraordinary appetite for hard work and unswerving dedication in support of the company's position.

Young says his enthusiasm for our prospects was genuine.

'When you think about the resources of Queensland and the location of your business – it blew me away that that sort of opportunity existed anywhere in the world still,' Young says. 'It was going to be a home run.'

We also organised a pivotal phone conference in November 2009 between Premier Bligh and Paul Martin, the former Canadian Prime Minister.

'The discussion with Paul Martin was important,' Hockridge says. 'It just happened at the right time. Doug had done his thing with the Treasurer, the Transport Minister and others. But for the then Finance Minister, subsequently Prime Minister, subsequently leader of the G20, to take quality time to talk to the Premier and Treasurer in clear and unequivocal terms both from a business point of view but also from a political point of view, I judged to have a very significant impact. I would have thought in the Premier's mind at the time there was no clear answer. To have Paul Martin speak in such a considered, powerful way struck a responsive chord that helped to draw together all those threads.'

Certain features of the CN deal were designed to make it more appealing to the voting public. Legislation guaranteed that the CN head office would be permanently in Montreal. The Canadians provided discounted share offers for employees and Canadians. They also imposed a 15 per cent cap on individual share ownership, to guard against a takeover by American interests.

Instead of a trade sale negotiated behind closed doors with large corporate bidders, there was emerging the prospect of a transparent transaction with special benefits for QR employees and Queensland residents.

By the last week of November 2009, we had done just about all we could. The government had received all of our analysis, they had spoken to their political counterparts in Canada, and they had the benefit of the sage advice from Australia's former ACCC head. Of course, they were hearing a very different story from the miners, Asciano and the Federal Government. It was now up to them to make the call.

············

Hockridge was invited to a meeting with the Premier and Treasurer on the night of 7 December 2009.

'The Premier said to me "Well Lance, there are so many people telling me what I should and shouldn't do, and whatever I do is going to disappoint a great deal of people, so I might as well do what I think is right,"' Hockridge recalls.

The next day, the government announced that the privatisation of QR National would involve a vertically integrated IPO, and it would be fast-tracked. Instead of the original three to five year timeframe, the sale would be completed by the end of 2010. The company was expected to be a top 50 listed company on the Australian Securities Exchange, and would be headquartered in Brisbane. Every employee would be gifted $1000 worth of shares, and Queenslanders would be given preference in the retail side of the transaction. And, to complete the familiar suite of features, individual shareholdings would be capped at 15 per cent. The Treasurer says he progressively changed his mind on the QRN structure during the months of the scoping study.

'Treasury's view was always inclined towards separation, but through the process I began to form the view that integration was a much better option,' he says.

'Sometimes governments can be guilty of slavishly sticking to a position when there are compelling reasons to move on. I didn't want to observe the conceit of sticking to the first proposals when there was an obviously more compelling transaction design.'

As Fraser saw it, the integrated sale structure was going to be the best way to reform QR.

'For me, the main reason was the capital issue that was the driver,' he says. 'But it had happily attached to it the capacity for QR National to change, grow and reform into the future and provide the ultimate security for its workforce. And, of course, a capacity to guarantee its role in contributing to the development of Queensland's economy. No one, not even the critics of the decision, would argue that change was not needed.'

From Fraser's perspective, the aggressive commerciality of QR's competitors – and the customers who were shaping up as competitors – would mean a bleak future for QR if there was not major change.

'It was only going to mean that in ten, fifteen years' time, maybe shorter, a much harder question was going to be in front of the managers and employees at QR,' he says.

On any analysis, the government's December announcement was a remarkable turnaround from June. The QR privatisation team was pleased with every aspect of the decision, except for one. The government had decided it would retain a cornerstone stake of between twenty-five and forty per cent. We anticipated this would be a drag on the float price, and create an uncertainty into the future. Still, it was a considerable achievement to move the government so significantly from their original plan. What we didn't realise was the battle had only just begun.

CHAPTER TEN

Breaking up is hard to do

If the enterprise agreement of February 2009 was a difficult period for the unions, then the IPO announcement in December 2009 sent them into deep shock. Instead of 1,000 QR employees going into the private sector, the proposed new structure would instead mean 9,000 making the change. And almost unbelievably to many unionists, the iconic workshops in Townsville, Rockhampton and Ipswich, would be part of the mix.

In the QR management camp, there was only a momentary pause to reflect on the enormity of the December decision.

'Since that awakening about the realities of politics, I had a high degree of scepticism about whether it could be achieved,' O'Toole says. 'It was good news but my first thought was how much we would have to do to make it stick.'

Mike Carter says moving the Government away from the 'carve it up and sell it off' model was a fantastic achievement.

'But we knew at the time there would be a bunch of people wanting to stop it, so our focus quickly changed to getting it done and getting it done quickly,' he says.

•••••••••••

Despite the exhaustion across the QR management team, there was to be no R&R, or time for reflection. The first order of business was to complete the separation of the freight business from the government passenger business.

The scale of what needed to happen was immense. The goal was to create two large-scale, functioning railway organisations out of one. The first, QR National, would be freight-specific and privatised via an IPO in November 2010. The second, Queensland Rail, would remain in government ownership, with its 6,500 employees focused chiefly on the passenger business, although it would retain the non-coal freight network as well.

The announcement took us straight into the Christmas holiday period. Many people in business and government disappeared for their annual holidays. At QR, however, as O'Toole recalls, the privatisation team moved urgently to map out the plan for separating QR National from Queensland Rail.

'It was crucial that we came straight out of the blocks on this,' O'Toole says.

Hundreds of inter-company agreements and contracts would need to be negotiated, millions of hectares of real estate would need to be divided, and complex information technology systems would need to be split. But most importantly, every employee would need to be allocated into positions in one company or the other. And each employee had to be consulted about this proposed change.

'Our overriding principle was that we needed to set up both entities for success,' QR's human resources head, John Stephens, recalls.

Stephens says the human resources and line management teams across the organisation set to work allocating employees based on what had been decided would be required for both entities. Where functions needed to be split, the teams went through a detailed capability assessment, and made sure that each organisation had what it needed.

'It was an enormous job,' he says. 'And it inevitably meant that QRN would lose some good people to Queensland Rail, and vice versa.'

Stephens says that there were some very specific strategic reasons for moving quickly on the separation.

'We did not want there to be an opportunity for the unions to stop the process,' he says. 'In our strategy, we figured that if we didn't move as soon as possible, and then consult with the unions at the latest stage, then we believed they would have procrastinated and that not only would the separation have not been done effectively, it would not have been done at all.'

The separation was a dimension beyond anything attempted with other privatised railroads, including those overseas. For example, Canadian National had been separated from its passenger cousin more than 10 years before its IPO. An Australian example from the airline industry involved Qantas and Australian Airlines were merged many years before privatisation. Uniquely, QR was being asked to pull off one of the biggest demergers in Australian history, and simultaneously orchestrate a ground-breaking IPO.

Hockridge and O'Toole were both meant to be on annual leave but instead they spent their holiday period in the office or on the phone dealing with the separation work. The entire human resources team, led by John Stephens, was in the same boat.

'I was quite resentful at the time because we were all exhausted and we all needed that holiday break,' O'Toole says. 'But our people worked like dogs to create the separated structure as quickly as we could.'

When the separation process was launched, the unions, along with most of Queensland, were on holidays. They had planned to recommence their campaign of action against asset sales early in the new year. This campaign had involved demonstrations in regional areas, television and newspaper advertising. What it didn't involve, however, was any meaningful contact with QR management, despite repeated approaches from us. The unions refused to discuss any aspect of the privatisation with QR, because they felt it would undermine their campaign of outright opposition.

As a result, the unions were wrong-footed when QR management managed to construct much of the fabric of separation over the Christmas holidays. They essentially had left themselves with no role in the separation process.

In allocating employees between companies, one of the critical questions was the starting point. Were we moving employees from or to the government entity? In the end it was felt it would be far less complicated to start with every employee in QR Limited (which would ultimately become QR National), and then transfer across the people needed for the new government railway.

Brendon Gibson, the former QR Treasurer who was now working full-time on the privatisation process, says this was a very important tactical move.

'It was smart to put everyone in QRN, and then ask them to jump back into government,' Gibson says. 'If we had done it the other way, it would have been harder. Imagine if we'd had 500 saying no – it could have impacted on the whole strategy.'

············

With military precision, the first part of the process was completed in a few weeks at the start of 2010. There were very few complaints or challenges from employees. But not everyone was happy. The unions took QR to the Federal Court, and in late June only a week before the officially scheduled date of separation, the company was fined $660,000 for breaching workplace laws (this sum was later reduced on appeal).

Federal Justice John Logan admonished QR for not providing employees with an opportunity to discuss if they would be moved into the private business, how that would occur, or if they wanted privatisation at all.

'It is truly radical change,' he said in his judgment. 'It is obvious change, change that was obviously intended to be the subject of consultation, and not to appreciate that, is to close one's eyes to the obvious.'[33]

The court ruled that the company 'utterly' failed to properly consult the workers over its privatisation plans. But there was no order to backtrack, or stop the separation process.

Disappointed as he was by the ruling, Stephens breathed a sigh of relief.

'The worst outcome for us would have been to have the process stopped, and to have to go back to the start and consult all over again,' he says. 'So I was pleasantly surprised that their case was about ineffective consultation rather than the separation itself.'

At the same time, Stephens was unhappy that QR lost the case.

'We had consulted more, in terms of talking to employees than anything I had been involved in before,' Stephens says. 'We held numerous face to face meetings with groups of employees throughout Queensland, including those chaired by the CEO, by the CEOs Direct Reports or by other senior management. In addition employees were provided with power point presentations, individual letters, memos, paper and electronic updates.'

Employees were able to ask questions, make suggestions or provide any other feedback to us. Nothing was off the table. Employees were able to provide this feedback verbally, in writing or electronically, including directly to the CEO. Ultimately ninety-eight per cent of the 3,600 employees who were offered a transfer to the new government railway accepted the offer.

'We were very thorough and that is why the decision was so disappointing,' Stephens says.

The court decision was undoubtedly a blow for the company, and caused renewed tensions with the government. Stephens was the man in the firing line.

'I was hauled before Treasurer Fraser to explain the outcome, and to say he was upset was an understatement,' he recalls.

Despite the bitter taste from the court decision, however, Stephens has few regrets about the process.

'If I had my time again, yes I would have changed some of the consultation aspects,' he says. 'But not in terms of timing, or our approach to engaging our employees directly. Because that would have meant we wouldn't have achieved the separation, and wouldn't have got to IPO in November.'

The other positive of the first part of the separation process was that it again demonstrated the ability of the team to tackle a seemingly impossible deadline and make it happen. This would set the tone for the rest of the separation work, with an important caveat. Nothing else must be allowed to go wrong.

···········

After the employee allocations had been completed, there was still much work to do on separating the organisations. Two teams, one in QRN and one in Queensland Rail, were established to work on the myriad remaining issues. Colin Keel, an American with a background in the airline industry, came late into the QR adventure, but very quickly found himself alongside Brendon Gibson working on separation and then bringing home Australia's second largest IPO.

Keel brought a structured approach, and some rather quirky metaphors. As far as Keel was concerned, large volume tasks, like the service contracts with Queensland Rail, could be imagined as pieces of work in a factory. Each piece of work had a factory manager from Keel's team.

'We had to figure out what its assembly line looked like, and we needed to work through a dashboard so that as factory manager they could understand what was going on,' Keel says. 'So I would continually ask – is your factory crumbling or is it pumping out the widgets like it should?'

Keel says that despite the degree of difficulty, people working on this exercise rarely lost their motivation for the fight. As he saw it, the team didn't need to keep reminding themselves that this was a defining moment in the history of the company.

'There were enough people on the team who were passionate, and really believed in what we were doing, that it carried the rest of the group,' he says. 'If you couldn't get swept up in it, then you were probably going to leave.'

There is some speculation that O'Toole was exercising her darkest sense of humour when she teamed up Gibson and Keel to manage the separation and IPO process. The diplomatic but resolute Keel would have his moments with the blunt and sometimes outrageous Gibson, but they would ultimately settle into a productive equilibrium.

On the Queensland Rail side, the head of the QR passenger business, Paul Scurrah, led the charge. Scurrah was no stranger to corporate upheaval, having been at the heart of the unsuccessful efforts to rescue Australia's Ansett airlines in the early 2000s. Scurrah set up a mirror Project Management Office to the QRN team and they set to work on the thousands of agreements that would be required to make the transition possible. At the time of the QR separation, Scurrah had not been confirmed as the new CEO of Queensland Rail so he must have felt he was in the middle of a long job interview. But people were working so hard that those considerations were not front of mind.

'It was bloody hard,' Scurrah says. 'Probably the most intense challenge I've ever been involved with, even taking into account Ansett. From December 8 through to June 30 was seven months and in the private world most people would have needed at least 12 months. By comparison, we've just had the 10th anniversary of the Ansett collapse and we are now only seeing the finalisation of the liquidation. So that's 10 years versus seven months.'

In all, the QR separation involved the renegotiation of more than 200 contracts, the allocation of 108,000 assets and the split between entities of more than 1600 information systems and applications.[34]

On top of the actual volume of work, the teams also had to deal with the very public nature of what they were doing.

'The unions were looking out for us to slip up every minute, then you had the newspapers, particularly *The Courier Mail*, constantly looking for the cracks as well,' Scurrah says. 'That they found very little is a great compliment to everyone.'

Despite the intensity, there were some amusing, some might say bizarre, bones of contention.

'The hottest issue was who would own Rail Centre One, the company headquarters,' Scurrah recalls. 'I could totally understand why it would have been logical for it to end up with QRN. And I could also understand the government not wanting to give up a piece of real estate above the rail corridor. The great thing is that Lance and I are very pragmatic about everything. Neither of us was overly sensitive about these issues that could otherwise have dealt with in turf war fashion. With RC1, it was really out of our hands in the end, because both the bankers and the government took over the issue. We just weren't going to get perfection so we agreed to move forward.'

It seems that there is no such thing as a new issue. The privatisation process for Canadian National in 1995 had involved a similar arm-wrestle over the ownership of a range of real estate assets, including the CN Tower in Toronto. In that case, the State also won the debate and retained ownership. Unlike CN, however, QR did not have any particularly odd property assets.

Many column inches have been devoted to the story of CN's ownership of a swanky hotel in Paris, which apparently was necessary so that managers of the Canadian railroad could always find accommodation when they attended UIC meetings in the French capital.

The other two major conundrums for the QR separation were an ongoing travel management contract, and free rail travel passes for employees. As part of the separation agreement, Queensland Rail wanted QR National to transfer most of its travel booking activity to the newly created Queensland Rail owned travel agency, Travel4. QRN explored other options, but in the end agreed to stay with Travel4.

Many of us with some experience in rail knew that employee rail passes would grab a disproportionate degree of attention. All QR employees enjoyed free rail travel in Queensland, which provided a useful commuting benefit for those in cities like Brisbane, and a treat for the families who wanted to ride the long distance passenger trains during the holidays. The same issue arose during the privatisation of National Rail Corporation and Freightcorp – would employees still get free rail travel, for how long, and who would pay? Even today, a number of private rail operators in Australia are still dealing with legacy passenger travel passes for employees.

In the whirlwind of separation activity, it is surprising that those who lived through it can identify only a few issues that were not handled well. One of the key banking advisors for the privatisation, the CBA's Leon Allen, nominated a frustrating delay in finalising accounts.

'It was difficult to get information,' Allen says. 'For example, to get capital spending numbers you had to go back to each business and you would have issues with legacy systems that aren't easily overcome. But at the time, that was the best that could be done.'

Gibson said the management committee meetings were too random, leaving some in his team exposed and having to make individual calls on big decisions.

'We were making many quick decisions, which you didn't have the time to refer up,' he says. 'We were having to ask ourselves "Is this in the best interests of the corporation?" You would just make a commercial call and move on to the next one.'

Gibson also says there were some issues that were addressed too late in the schedule, like the need for extra legal resources, and a comprehensive plan for the separation of IT systems.

'We didn't start work on this until February/March but in the end we patched our way through,' Gibson says. 'The first pay went through OK, which was a good outcome because the Queensland Health payroll crisis was happening at the same time.'

O'Toole gives the team a little more credit for managing the systems transition.

'Did anything miss a beat?' she says. 'Did the payroll fall over? Did we have any customers complain? Did any system go down? I thought people did a really good job on both sides with a whole lot of really tough issues.'

Scurrah believes the best measure of the success of the separation was the lack of interest in it.

'We knew we had to get the fundamentals right,' he says. 'We had to have our safety accreditation nailed so that we had passenger and freight trains operating on July 1. It was hugely important that we didn't get distracted on our safety journey, or lose focus on our customers. My guys were actually put out, because QR National was getting all the publicity. But that was actually a compliment for us. Safety improved, that's no story. Customers are happy, that's no story. We're actually going to deliver the dividend we promised to government – that's no story.'

CHAPTER ELEVEN

We will destroy your IPO

After Premier Bligh's 8 December 2009 announcement, the mining industry went into overdrive. As the mining companies saw it, the government had buckled to the short term, do-the-deal advice from their merchant bankers. The proposed IPO would, according to Queensland Resources Council (QRC) CEO Michael Roche 'perpetuate a model that had previously locked out competition from Queensland's coal business.' QR's major competitor Asciano called for the ACCC to 'closely review' the transaction. Business columnist for *The Australian*, Matthew Stevens, opined 'Bligh has delivered herself an open invitation to a State Government Hall of Infrastructure Infamy.'[35]

We expected a temporary bath in the media, but were treated instead to a relentless military-style campaign, both public and private. Momentarily wrong-footed, the mining companies adjusted expertly and were soon orchestrating the debate.

During the scoping study period, the government had contemplated transferring the network to the Federal Government track manager, the ARTC. This would have mirrored the approach in New South Wales, where both general freight and coal lines had been taken over by the ARTC. The Hunter Valley was operating satisfactorily and there had been substantial Federal Government investment in system expansion.

An ARTC takeover would have had the support of most of the coal industry. However, ARTC had no experience of a running a narrow gauge tropical railroad, and an inter-government transfer to ARTC would have done little to address the financial problems facing Queensland. The State would also still have been left with the challenge of what to do with the remaining QR freight organisation. An alternative plan, under which the ARTC would take over the non-coal network in Queensland, had been rejected by the ARTC.

BHP Billiton reacted very quickly to the IPO announcement. Courtesy of *The Australian* journalist Matthew Stevens, who was to get a whole year of material out of the QR National issue, it became publicly known that BHP had gone it alone and approached the government with a new proposal for it to buy the coal track, and sub-lease it to the ARTC.[36] This bid did not have the support of the other miners, who were concerned about their rival seizing control of the network.

The QR National privatisation team was a little surprised that BHP was putting so many resources into opposing the IPO plan. After all, the world's biggest mining company had many other interests across the world, and was involved in a number of expansions and potential acquisitions that dwarfed the value of the QRN coal network. But looking back on the episode today, the BHP move was entirely rational, and strategically logical.

As we have seen, QR had not historically operated efficiently or commercially. But the industry had always had some level of certainty about capital investment, because it was underwritten by government, and Queensland Governments of all persuasions had been more than willing to invest in growth. A privatised QR National, however, was an unknown – it was not clear how the new process would deliver the expansion tonnes.

For a company like BHP, with its metallurgical coal business in particular entirely dependent on the QR National network, this was clearly seen as a strategic risk. In addition, BHP had been seeking a greater level of control over all of its key supply chains. And finally, they were galvanised by the testy nature of some of QR's previous dealings with BHP.

We recognised, therefore, that it was really up to QRN to demonstrate that we had the vision and capability to be a genuine partner in BHP's coking and thermal coal growth plans. And we needed to make sure that companies like BHP were unrestricted if they wanted to fund, build or own their own expansion infrastructure.

Looking ahead at the significant growth opportunities in Queensland coal, Hockridge was very relaxed about the involvement of others in rail infrastructure. As he has now said on a number of occasions, 'We don't expect to do everything.' In fact, the QR National/Aurizon view was, and is, that there is scope and genuine benefit in other players coming into the system.

The trouble was that the industry simply didn't believe Hockridge was genuine about this. They thought that our 'user funding' alternatives would not work in practice, and that QRN would find a way of blocking or delaying key parts of the process to ensure that companies eventually agreed to QRN control of projects. So designing a user funding system that was not open to gaming was going to be a critical task. This was all part of our thinking in the early days following the IPO announcement.

In the meantime, BHP continued its counter-offensive. The BHP-only proposal was rejected quickly by the Treasurer, who told media that the government had already considered a range of options, and had now made its 'final decision'.

The boss of the Queensland Resources Council (QRC) Michael Roche was adamant that the IPO could not be allowed to go ahead.

'We must change their minds,' he told *The Australian Financial Review*. 'It is a must for the industry that this integrated business, initial public offering, does not proceed as currently proposed.'[37]

Macarthur Coal CEO Nicole Hollows, whose company had recently moved to contract all of their Queensland haulage with QRN's competitor PN/Asciano, described the float structure as the 'worst possible scenario'.

'If you really wanted to create competition, the above rail should have been floated, and not the below rail. How does having them both actually create competition?' she said.[38]

Again, the focus of the public comments was on the issue of competition, not investment. Yet, one of the bizarre sub-plots in the immediate aftermath of Premier Bligh's IPO announcement on QR National was the growing call for Asciano to bid for QR's 'above rail' assets as a tactical spoiler move.[39] To his credit the then CEO of Asciano Mark Rowsthorn was quick to dismiss this option. But it was still instructive that some in the debate were prepared to countenance a scenario under which two coal rail haulage operators would be dissolved into one.

············

In the first few days after Premier Bligh's IPO announcement, it was clear QR National would be in an ongoing battle for our existence. Within the privatisation team, we recognised that we were exposed because we had few natural allies, other than the government itself. We were successful in gaining some initial support from groups like the Australian Industry Group and Infrastructure Partnerships Australia. We learned later that both groups made themselves extremely unpopular with the mining lobby by proffering support for the IPO.

The mining lobby, however, realised that in addition to maintaining the rage in a public debate, it needed a credible alternative to the IPO plan. The BHP solo idea was gone, but BHP worked hard to re-establish the consortium of companies that had knocked on the government's door during the scoping study period. The new group would become known as the Queensland Coal Industry Rail Group (QCIRG).

On 11 December 2009, just three days after the government's IPO announcement, the new consortium delivered a 'formal' offer to buy the coal network. This was no knee-jerk response. It quickly emerged that the miners had been exploring plans to acquire the QR coal network since Premier Bligh's initial asset sale announcement in June 2009. Despite offer details being 'scant', Matthew Stevens and other commentators observed that the miners' bid was seen as superior by Asciano, the Federal Government, the ARTC and had even received 'private' support from the ACCC.[40] The mining companies had been breathtakingly successful in amassing this level of third party support so quickly. Stevens made this bold statement about the expected ACCC comfort with the miners' model:

'Given that the plan would create a more independent and transparent management of the rail network than currently exists, it is very hard to see how the change would trigger the "no lessening of competition" thresholds that determine regulatory objection.'[40]

One difficulty for the mining consortium was that while pressure could be brought to bear by powerful third parties, the ultimate decision still lay with the Queensland Government. Some were also making the mistake of assuming that the ACCC would be involved in any regulatory oversight of a privatised QRN. That would be the job of Queensland's home-grown regulator, the Queensland Competition Authority (QCA).[41]

Despite this, the mining companies had established head-spinning momentum. And they were further buoyed by the entry to the debate of Nick Greiner. Greiner had been successful in brokering a peace deal between mining companies in the Hunter Valley who were finding it difficult to agree on port allocations. All the major players had confidence in Greiner's ability. For example, Hubie van Dalsen, head of BHP's coal business, had seen Greiner in action directly when he ran Rio Tinto's Hunter Valley operations during the reform years.

A feature of the Hunter Valley breakthrough had been the way that Greiner had helped the larger and smaller players to find common ground in the overall interests of the supply chain. This skill would be crucial to brokering industry agreement on a plan for the Central Queensland coal network.

BHP and the mining consortium employed Greiner to front the negotiations with government on their behalf. Greiner was also Chair of Citibank in Australia, which took on the financial management of the consortium bid. Unflappable, with an instinct for newsy one-liners, he was also a highly credible public face for the campaign.

Shortly after these developments, QR booked a table at the high profile Infrastructure Partnerships Australia National Awards Dinner in Sydney. Hosted by our Chair John Prescott, we were entertaining a number of senior Australian business figures, including Asciano Chair Malcolm Broomhead and Toll Holdings Chair Ray Horsburgh. Nick Greiner was there and Hockridge approached him to say hello as a courtesy. While they shook hands, Greiner lent forward and said, 'We will destroy your IPO.'

At the start of 2010, it was hard to tell how much traction the mining consortium bid would get. But we knew that we needed to be more proactive in defending our position.

There were two key elements to our new strategy – shift the onus of proof to our opponents, and take the argument out of the Australian context. Our narrative would be that while our model was tested, and had performed both locally and globally, the alternatives proposed were experimental and risky. For both customers and policy makers, our message was that the stakes were too high to take this risk.

Unfortunately, we were starting from a long way behind with some stakeholders. For example, direct QRN liaison with the Federal Government was considered off-limits, because that was a relationship being managed by the Queensland Government. Of course there was some reason to expect that the Federal Government would be a silent bystander. Normally, you would have expected a Federal Labor Government to allow a Queensland Labor Government the freedom to dispose of its own assets as it saw fit. Even if some Federal individuals had entertained private misgivings, you would normally expect that their public position would be 'it's a matter for the State.'

The Federal Government at the time was led by first-term Prime Minister Kevin Rudd, himself a Queenslander. Rudd was still riding high in the polls two years after a landslide election that had swept away the long-running conservative Howard Government.

Within months of Premier Bligh's IPO announcement, we were astonished to see several Federal Ministers place on the public record their concerns and in some cases, outright opposition to the IPO plan. Resources and Energy Minister and former union leader Martin Ferguson led the charge. At first, he was subtle and indirect, expressing confidence 'in private rail corridors in WA and increasing confidence in the Hunter Valley', while confessing he had a 'huge issue' with some developments in Queensland.[42] Some time later, the language was more colourful. 'The Queensland model in my opinion is a recipe for disaster,' Minister Ferguson told *The 7.30 Report*.[43]

One month after Ferguson's intervention, Federal Finance Minister Lindsay Tanner and Infrastructure Minister Anthony Albanese[44] both made public comments critical of the QR National privatisation model.

And finally Federal Treasurer Wayne Swan issued his own gentle criticism, although he was careful to stop short of actual opposition to the Bligh Government move.

'Federal politicians took a position in isolation of the facts and jumped the gun early,' QR National/Aurizon's head of Corporate Affairs Paul Cronin says. 'Minister Ferguson was convinced by the coal companies, whereas Albanese had been influenced by the experiences of privatisation closer to home. He wasn't aware of the Class 1 experience. We left it too late to try to bring them on board.'

The rapid success of the miners with politicians was no surprise to John Stephens.

'As a former executive with BHP, I knew their influence, how they could get to both Federal and State, and frankly I was worried,' Stephens says. 'The coal companies built up a lot of momentum, and it is so rare to see them united on anything, because normally they are so strongly against each other.'

While the procession of critical Federal Ministers was a concern, Cronin says it never reached crisis proportions.

'I think if you'd lost Swan and Rudd, that would have been a game-changer, because of their positions, and the fact they are both Queenslanders,' he says. 'We understand that Swan and Rudd both had misgivings, but did not go public with them.'

Despite the urgings of the Queensland Government for QRN to stay out of the conversation with the Federal Government, we started a belated dialogue with the relevant Federal Departments, and Ministers Ferguson and Albanese. It was helpful in providing overall context to policy makers, even if it did not sway the positions of the Ministers.

The most compelling part of our message was that we were able to talk specifically about the investment pipeline in Queensland coal. Mine growth plans meant that it was not unthinkable that Queensland coalfields would see rail investments of up to $18 billion over a ten-year period. We had assessed and prioritised these potential investments. Our message was that QRN would be established with a strong balance sheet, intimate knowledge of the investment and operating environment, and immediate capability to get on with the job of enabling growth. By virtue of our integration, which meant we stood to earn returns both 'below rail' and 'above rail', we had a greater incentive to make the investments. We also believed we had the strongest incentive to make investments that benefited all miners – large and small, existing and new.

This was the kind of argument that we put to Minister Ferguson, who by this time was also focussed on the issue of investment. However, it was evident that he had developed a clear position and would not be moved. The clincher for him was the mining consortium setting aside $2.05 billion to underpin QRN's capital plan. Our $3 billion credit facility was to provide the same kind of mechanism.

'I am not confident the Queensland Government's model will deliver the necessary investment,' he told *The 7.30 Report*.

The mining consortium bid was taking shape, and was formally launched after a meeting convened by Greiner in March 2010. Thirteen companies had joined the group, among them the Federal Government's track organisation the ARTC. It was not clear at this stage, however, what kind of equity commitment had been made by the ARTC.

The QCIRG offer had four goals: to encourage fair and open access, optimise network performance, enable early system expansions, and encourage rail haulage competition, all with flow-on benefits through enhanced investment, employment and royalties. By March 2010, Nick Greiner was sensing the momentum was shifting towards QCIRG. He adopted a more direct tone in media comments, and was openly critical of the Queensland Treasurer for not running a 'dual track' sale process.

'It's banking 101, it's auction 101,' he told *The 7.30 Report*. 'If you've got a house to sell you try and get more than one person to buy so you get the best price.'[43]

And when asked his reaction to the Treasurer casting doubt over whether a formal, binding bid would ever eventuate, Greiner was direct.

'The Queensland Treasurer, with great respect, is making it up,' Greiner said. 'He's blowing wind. ... He must think that people have got nothing better to do. It really is trivial and I've been trying to avoid getting into a slanging match with a Treasurer whom I've never met. But frankly, he doesn't do himself any good by trying to make it a political bun fight.'[43]

In some ways, the clash was taking on the more familiar tone of a typical political stoush. Some saw this as an inevitable result of pitting an ex-Liberal Premier against a State Labor Government.

'If you're trying to influence a State Labor Government, don't appoint an ex-Liberal Premier,' Paul Cronin says. 'Straight away you're off to a bad start.'

Matt Keenan also thought it was an odd choice.

'It was quite bizarre that the coal companies thought the best way to influence a Labor Premier is to send in an ex-Liberal Premier from another State,' he says. 'And what's more, that State is Queensland's mortal enemy in the annual State of Origin football clashes.'

Treasurer Andrew Fraser knew he was obliged to engage with Greiner, although he was still unsure of the exact motives behind the QCIRG bid. However, before his first meeting with Greiner and QCIRG, he was to receive a very bad signal.

As Fraser stopped by Premier Bligh's office, before walking with her to the meeting, he received a phone call from his office. ABC radio was asking for comment about the outcome of the meeting, which of course, had not even started. Fraser's office replied that the meeting had not yet happened, and were told that ABC already had comment from Greiner about the meeting. *The Australian Financial Review* was also running similar comments from Greiner in an online story.

'To me that signalled that he [Greiner] in particular was going to be more politician than commercial banker,' Fraser says. 'I was always prepared to deal with him, as with anyone else, in a genuinely commercial manner. But it was clear to me from that point onwards that he was going to be a political, rather than commercial participant, and I thereafter discounted his role.'

As a result, the relationship between Fraser and Greiner was to be rather frosty. On several occasions, Greiner was publicly dismissive of Fraser's abilities, and questioned his basic competence. After Greiner's 'banking 101' comment, Fraser mused that Greiner was 'like the dog that has caught a taxi, he doesn't know what to do now.' It was getting personal.

Mike Carter was very unfortunate to get caught in the crossfire of this tension. He, Deb O'Toole and Brendon Gibson were in Sydney for a meeting with BHP to talk about the float, when Greiner walked in. Greiner mistook Carter and Gibson for missionaries from Queensland Treasury, and regaled them about Fraser's dog comment, before suggesting he bring a bone to the next meeting with Fraser to 'shove it down his throat.'

'He calmed down a bit when he heard we were from QR National,' Carter says.

While QCIRG were not getting the royal treatment yet from the Queensland Government, it was a very different story in Canberra. Greiner was successfully co-opting Labor Cabinet Ministers, one at a time. Towards the middle of 2010, Greiner claimed that 'we'll soon have half the Federal Cabinet on side.'[45]

The mining industry's relationship with the Federal Government by then had become very complicated. In May 2010, Prime Minister Kevin Rudd had announced a new Super Profits Resource Tax on mining. Mining companies launched a furious counter attack, complete with dramatic national television advertisements. Prime Minister Rudd and Treasurer Wayne Swan returned fire, dismissing the campaign as self-interested and unpatriotic. Swan would later write in *The Monthly*:

'A handful of vested interests that have pocketed a disproportionate share of the nation's economic success now feel they have a right to shape Australia's future to satisfy their own self-interest.'[46]

The twist was that while the miners were finding common ground with the Federal Government on the QR National privatisation, they were locked in mortal struggle around the mining tax. There were times when we feared our coal network could end up becoming a consolation prize for the miners.

Then Federal politics became a national soap opera. At one time the most popular Prime Minister in Australian history, Kevin Rudd was spectacularly removed by his Deputy Julia Gillard on 24 June 2010. It was the first time that a PM had been removed by his own party during his first term of government. The new Prime Minister claimed that the Rudd Government had 'lost its way' and pledged action to fix three key issues – the mining tax, carbon pricing and the country's policy towards asylum seekers.

Some saw this extraordinary episode as a mark of the power of special interest groups, including the mining lobby. And it was instructive that one of the immediate actions of Prime Minister Julia Gillard involved the effective watering down of the mining tax. At QR National, we looked for clues about impacts on our IPO. Would Gillard have a view about our IPO? Could we be part of the mining tax trade-off?

Our conclusion, and hope, was that the dramatic events of June 2010 would mean there were bigger issues for the 'Feds' to confront than a railway privatisation in Queensland.

CHAPTER TWELVE

Communication breakdown

As we had learned from the Canadian National experience, the marketing of a reformist government is critical to its success. Unfortunately, the Queensland Government was slow out of the blocks in December 2009, and when it did communicate, its messages were missing the mark. Matt Keenan believes they were concentrating on the wrong reasons for selling an asset like QR National.

'We really wanted to focus on the real issues, not that the Government was selling to address credit rating issues,' Keenan says. 'The real message was that a government owning a commercial railway competing with commercial operators and dealing with commercial coal companies, was nuts.'

The then Economics Editor of *The Australian* Michael Stutchbury, mining the same rhetorical vein as Doug Young's pioneering privatisation of CN, showed the Premier how a simple economic message could work for the QR National privatisation.

'Her [Bligh's] Queensland Government has enough on its hands running hospitals and schools and accommodating the State's population boom,' Stutchbury wrote.

'The private sector is better placed to raise the risk capital to expand and run the efficient rail operations needed to maximise Queensland's mining exports and underpin the national economy's next growth phase.'[47]

Possibly influenced by the growing rebellion in her own party ranks, Bligh stopped short of this message clarity. The Premier immediately got into a tangle on the day of the IPO announcement by arguing that the 99-year lease of the QR National rail infrastructure did not represent a full privatisation.[48]

The one bright spot was that QR National was ensuring its local performance was squeaky clean. There would be no more Riverfire-style scandals.

'One of the best things we did was that we kept out of the front half of *The Courier Mail*,' Paul Cronin says. 'If we had been there, that would have engaged more of Caucus, more of the unions. We managed issues well, and put out all the bushfires.'

In national media, however, QR National was being clearly out-gunned. The government had chosen to run its own communications strategy, and although the QR National team could see that the campaign needed more resources, and a more national scope, the government was slow to act.

'It took a long time to get a PR firm appointed, and as a result, the opponents of the process occupied the territory,' Keenan says. 'We were keen to get them involved early but it only happened late in the piece and frankly by the time they arrived, they were playing catch up with very well organised lobbyists.'

The agency was Sydney-based Kreab Gavin Anderson, and they did a reasonable job in difficult circumstances. The privatisation team worked hard to create angles for them, achieving some success, but it was small compared to the mining company onslaught.

QCIRG was playing a very sophisticated game. This was driven home to me when they forced the Federal Department of Infrastructure to release its advice critical of QRN under a Freedom of Information request.

In addition to Federal Government Ministers, QCIRG had convinced economists and even agricultural peak bodies to oppose our model. A significant wakeup call was the change of position from one of our earlier supporters, Infrastructure Partnerships Australia. As indicated earlier, in December 2009, IPA's Executive Director Brendan Lyon had supported the IPO announcement, stating that 'the float of Queensland Rail's coal businesses will allow Queensland to fund its massive infrastructure backlog.'[49]

Yet two months later, Lyon penned an extraordinary attack on the QR National sale model in an opinion piece for *The Australian Financial Review*. Calling for full structural separation of QRN's track and train infrastructure, Lyon wrote 'Bligh needs to get this right. Floating QR National in its present form has the potential to dramatically stifle competition in a key market.'[50]

Along with Asciano, QR had been a long-standing member of the Tourism and Transport Federation, which was part of the IPA stable. We felt betrayed, and as we were now on a war footing, decided to immediately fight back. On the day the article appeared, Prescott, Hockridge and myself contacted all key IPA figures, including board members, to express our outrage and disappointment.

I took up the cudgel with Lyon, who was shocked by our reaction. He made the point that his real target was the Queensland Government and the policy mistake he believed it was making. I argued that his words were doing material damage to one of the key infrastructure groups in the country, and that he was dead wrong about the effects of the vertical integration model in Queensland.

At the time, Hockridge wrote a letter of response to the AFR that called on commentators to base their arguments in fact.

'QR supports competition and the transparent access regulation that delivers it,' he wrote. 'It is access, not structural separation, that creates competition. Rail access regulation in Queensland works, as evidenced by the recent entry and growth of Asciano in the Queensland market.'[51]

This only provided the briefest respite in the chorus against the QR sale model. In April 2010, *The Australian Financial Review* found space for another vertical separation plea from Mark Christensen. 'If the QR privatisation isn't redesigned,' Christensen wrote, 'Bligh and Fraser will be offering investors a share in an unsustainable corporate structure.'[52]

Our next move was to take our message to the most prestigious venue in Australia, the National Press Club. In front of more than 100 industry players and media, our Chair John Prescott mounted a comprehensive defence of the QR National float structure, describing it as a 'watershed event for the national economy.' Prescott discussed in detail the experience in North America with vertically integrated railroads, which were 'the most affordable in the world,' delivering rates that were half of their equivalent in China and Japan, and 50 to 75 per cent below those in major European countries.

Critics were unmoved.

'For all its quality,' wrote *The Australian*'s Matthew Stevens, 'the QR Chair's Press Club pitch for his railway to reputational redemption failed to deal with the most obvious issue: his customers, at almost every level, hate the plan and are pursuing options to scuttle it.'[53]

· · · · · · · · · · · ·

While Hockridge and Prescott were compelling presenters of the case for vertical integration, it was too easy for opponents to dismiss their words as self-interested. It was clear that we urgently needed to add new voices and angles to the debate. At the time, we had been considering another visit to North America, to learn more about the privatisation experiences for Canadian National and a USA example, Conrail. One idea was to take a small group of blue-collar employees across to speak to their counterparts about life under privatisation.

While this plan did not go ahead, we decided that I would return to the States with QR's Manager of Operational Excellence Lindsay Cooper. We spent time understanding reform strategies and change management at CN, Burlington Northern and CSX. When Cooper returned, he was able to share with hundreds of front line employees a vivid and compelling picture of the energy and opportunity a private sector railroad could bring.

I continued the search for potential advocates for our IPO position. In Washington DC, I spoke to the Policy and Government Affairs operatives at the

Association of American Railroads (AAR). With no significant background in the vertical separation/integration tussle, they found just the fact that we were having the debate difficult to fathom. And they were dumbstruck that a group of customers had mounted what was effectively a hostile takeover bid for the track. AAR's impressive President and CEO Ed Hamberger was so concerned by our situation that he wrote a passionate opinion piece for Australia media. This was sent by Hamberger to *The Australian Financial Review*, but for some reason it never appeared.

I also met a very seasoned economic analyst, Justin Zubrod, who had worked for many years for Booz and Company in DC. Zubrod has extensive global experience of railroad industry structures. In addition to many years of consulting to Class 1 North American railroads, Zubrod is also familiar with European separated structures, and even worked on the New Zealand rail privatisation. Zubrod wrote an opinion piece powerfully contrasting the impoverished European separation experience with the success of integration in North America. Again, this piece was not published by *The Australian Financial Review*.

A third opinion piece from North America also failed to excite Australian media gatekeepers. This drew on the experience of a senior commercial executive who had unusually held senior roles on both sides of the fence – as a railroad customer, and then as a railroad operations manager. He was able to speak about the practical advantages of an integrated structure.

In Boston, I spoke to a global expert in access regulation, Jose Gomez Ibanez, of the Kennedy School of Business at Harvard University. He was particularly interested in our situation as he was due to address the ACCC's Regulatory Conference on the Gold Coast later in 2010.

I gave him a thorough brief on the issues, and followed up with him when he arrived in Queensland. Terry Cutler was able to act as his minder during the Conference. In front of most of the key figures at the ACCC, Gomez Ibanez created quite a stir with a devastatingly effective defence of the vertical integration model. He spoke at length to a journalist from *The Australian Financial Review*, but the story never did get a run.

The day before I was due to leave the USA, I tracked down a former CEO of Burlington Northern, Darius Gaskins. Crammed into a semi-quiet corner on a mobile phone in a frantic Chicago airport terminal, I learned that Gaskins was a giant of the railroad industry, and also held a strong regulatory pedigree, having been Head of the Surface Transportation board for a number of years.

Gaskins travelled to Australia to advise QRN on its IPO plans, and address potential investors and Federal Government bureaucrats. He agreed to speak to media about his experiences, and could not resist some comments about the QR National privatisation debate.

Gaskins told *The Australian* that owning both above and below rail was 'necessary for the economics of the business and also to ensure rail freight services were available to a wide range of customers'.[54] He dismissed the separation proposal as a 'silly idea'. To my relief, this story actually made it into print (albeit not in *The Australian Financial Review*).

Interestingly, although the story again trawled over the structural and competition issues, it zeroed in on investment. Gaskins had been quick to see this as the central issue, and encouraged coal companies to 'begin talking with the organisation (QRN) about possibly jointly funding any investments to upgrade its coal hauling capacity'.

Another, more familiar visitor was Doug Young, who by now was providing ongoing advice to the privatisation team. He was not only a larger than life, colourful embodiment of what we could achieve, but also a savvy advisor on everything from dealing with government to wrestling with bankers.

Young also wrote an opinion piece that ran prominently in *The Australian*. Our success rate was improving. With an eye as much on the investment community as the decision-makers in the Queensland Government, Young wrote that the 'vertically integrated model inspires confidence'.[55] He chronicled the compelling evidence that demonstrated that, on any measure, the North American railroads were the most successful in the world. Vertical integration had delivered the lowest customer freight rates, the highest levels of investment, and the best safety outcomes.

'It has been repeatedly shown that a separated track operating on a regulated return does not provide the sufficient investment incentives that are needed to ensure the infrastructure is available to carry the increasing tonnages that will result from a mining boom,' he wrote.

As we have seen before, Young was not only helpful to our cause with the media. He also spent time with the political decision-makers in Queensland, QRN management and board members, and with the wider investment community. For example, Paul Cronin contacted Leon Allen at CBA to help organise a lunchtime forum with Young as guest speaker.

'We got the call and two weeks later we had 200 people at the Sofitel to hear him,' Allen says. 'He was a great salesman, and I think even just in the small community of Brisbane corporate types, they were saying, "Hang on a second, this is quite interesting, I want to hear more."'

Unfortunately, against the weight of the combined marketing and lobbying resources of the biggest coal companies in the world, these small wins were not denting the overall impression created by the media – that the mining bid was a no-brainer, and that Fraser and Bligh should capitulate. In particular, the stance of *The Australian Financial Review* was causing many raised eyebrows. Fraser was becoming increasingly concerned about the relentless position being taken by Australia's daily financial newspaper.

'I'm not a politician who will regularly engage with journalists or newspaper editors about my view of whether a story is right or wrong,' he says. 'But for me, the role that *The Australian Financial Review* played came close to breaking my heart. I think it's a worthwhile paper that has a serious role to play. I agree with its editorialising more often than not. For it to be actively campaigning against us because of Mr Greiner's relationship with the paper, I thought was tragically disappointing. I certainly rang the editor about the obvious way that they were facilitating Mr Greiner's political objectives.'

Young was also amazed at the partisan nature of the media coverage on QRN issues.

'It was the single-most disturbing aspect for me,' he says. 'Why wouldn't they look at experiences outside Australia? They just had to check with the World Bank, the OECD, and the North American railroads. The opponents of the sale didn't need to purchase advertising, because anything they produced would get printed. Anything we produced was a blip.'

While we were balancing up the debate to some extent, the momentum was still overwhelmingly with the mining companies. In mid May 2010, QCIRG announced they had secured full financing for their bid.[56] On 18 May, our main competitor Asciano declared that it had applied to have the QR coal network placed under federal control, adding another potential delay to our timeframes. Asciano CEO Mark Rowsthorn dismissed the diligent regulatory approach at the Queensland Competition Authority as 'weak and open to exploitation.'[57]

QR National and the government responded quickly to the opening of this new front. On 17 June, Premier Bligh applied to the National Competition Council to have the Queensland Rail Access Regime certified as an effective access regime. The Queensland Government and QR National prepared detailed submissions in support of this application.

In July, the German engineering and construction group Bilfinger Berger announced it was abandoning a plan to float its Australian division, Valemus, due to adverse market conditions. In an extraordinary irony, the Chair of Valemus at the time was none other than Nick Greiner.

Some saw the Valemus move as a potentially knockout blow for the QR National plan. Under the dramatic headline 'Valemus decision may kill QR rail offering', Mark Ludlow, a journalist with *The Australian Financial Review*, wrote 'the Valemus decision could provide a well-timed pause for thought for Premier Anna Bligh and her Treasurer Andrew Fraser.'[58]

Then in early August 2010, QCIRG sweetened their bid to $5.2 billion, on the proviso that they be allowed due diligence within two weeks. It was a clear effort to put pressure on the government before the federal election, which was to be held on 21 August. This antagonised the government, and the miners withdrew this condition almost immediately.

If we thought, however, that this would hold back QCIRG's progress, we were wrong.

On 11 August 2010, Hockridge received a call from the Treasurer to inform him that QCIRG would be allowed to conduct due diligence on the Central Queensland coal network. It was now a genuine two-horse race.

CHAPTER THIRTEEN

The final putsch

The State's decision to allow due diligence for the QCIRG bid was a bitter blow for us. First, it indicated that the IPO may not proceed. Secondly, if the IPO was ultimately chosen as the way forward, we were concerned that QCIRG due diligence would have given customers access to highly sensitive information that would erode our commercial position in the future.

For those of us who passionately believed in the IPO, this would be a difficult period.

Colin Keel, who with Brendon Gibson was driving the financial aspects of the separation and IPO, remembers that it was a Friday afternoon when O'Toole called him into her office, and told him they needed to talk about something absolutely confidential. O'Toole told him he would be moved temporarily from the IPO team to work on the due diligence for the miner's bid.

'That weekend was really hard for me, because I felt internally conflicted,' he says. 'I was well into the work on the IPO, and I really believed in this privatisation. But if we had put down the shutters, we would have lost control of the process that we had spent at least a year laying the foundations for. And it was just a critical point in time.'

Keel and a key expert from the Network business, Mark Bourdaniotis, set to work immediately on constructing the data room for QCIRG. QR National's Executive General Manager of Enterprise Services Greg Pringle was also involved in scoping and implementing the process.

'We worked systematically through the list and worked out what we could justifiably put into a data room, those things that we have some concerns about, and the red items that were off limits,' Keel says. 'Green, yellow and red – not rocket science.'

It was, however, a massive exercise. In the final analysis, Keel and his team compiled 9722 documents for the data room, and fielded 1287 due diligence questions from the State's legal advisors.

'Deb called me towards the end of the weekend and asked how I was doing,' Keel says. 'Not with the work, but as a person. That was really important because she understood the position I was in. I know I came out of that weekend having learned a lot about leadership. It was almost like an energy boost even though at the beginning it had been a tough nut to swallow.'

Greg Pringle says that the mining data room was a supreme test of QR National's professionalism.

'It required an act of will, both intellectually and ethically, not to pursue an agenda in which you had a vested interest,' Pringle says. 'You just had to draw on objective, dispassionate professionalism.'

Some of our team, like Paul Cronin, were more relaxed about the QCIRG due diligence decision.

'I wasn't as concerned as some about the due diligence,' Cronin says. 'With the companies having made the offer, I never thought the Government could just dismiss it out of hand. The coal company bid was genuinely live and had to be genuinely assessed'.

••••••••••••

In the lead up to Treasurer Fraser's decision to allow due diligence for the mining companies in August, we had sharpened our tactical approach. Rather than swing wildly at every angle, our coalition had decided to focus on two key areas of vulnerability for QCIRG. The first was the competition and transition implications of their bid. The second was our fundamentally different approach to communities and employment. These two angles drove our work from June 2010 through to the government's final decision in September.

As we have heard, the mining companies' consortium had reportedly received a positive hearing from the ACCC. In June, QCIRG had formally approached the Commission for a review of the bid. Some were expecting it to be a formality.

It was to be a short review. On 28 June, the ACCC gave interested parties just three weeks to submit a response. At that stage, there was nothing in the public domain other than a series of media releases from QCIRG.

The ACCC process was not high on the radar internally. We were unsure if the Queensland Government would be happy for us to participate in the review. We did not know if the government proposed to put in its own submission. In the end, we decided we needed to be part of the process, and it had to be a serious piece of work. Feeling particularly passionate about this issue, and its importance to our prospects, I volunteered to drive this response. I was given the green light and considerable autonomy to get the job done.

I worked closely with NERA Economic Consultants and our internal regulatory expert Dean Gannaway on a series of papers that looked into the competition issues raised by the proposed QCIRG acquisition. Terry Cutler, the brains trust player with the most regulatory experience, was also heavily involved.

We looked at all of the known precedents for user ownership of infrastructure. We explored the way Australian miners had worked together in the Hunter Valley. We also looked at the dynamics between the larger and smaller miners in Queensland.

Here we had been helped by the recent withdrawal of QCoal from QCIRG. With interests in five existing and potential mines in Queensland, QCoal was an impressive new player in Queensland coal, although it was still very much a minnow compared to BHP, Rio, Xstrata and Anglo.

This quartet was responsible for more than 70 per cent of the use of the Queensland coal network.

QCoal CEO Chris Wallin had launched a stinging criticism of the QCIRG model, telling *The Courier Mail*:

'Basically the model proposed is where the big companies will control the track and we will end up with one per cent and if you have ever owned one per cent of the shares in the company you will find out you do not get much say .... We also think that the proposal by the coal companies was inferior to the government model.'[59]

The consortium had been further weakened by the news that the mid-tier mining companies Aquila and New Hope would not be providing equity contributions, although they would remain 'supporting parties'.[60]

Mike Carter says while there were some cracks, the separation cause still galvanised most of the customers.

'They always struggle at getting it together,' Carter says. 'But I could see it in the eyes of some of them – this was the most aligned and determined that I had seen them for a long time. They had spent a lot of time trying to marshal all of the players.'

No matter how you looked at it, you could not escape the fact that there was no global precedent for what the miners were proposing. A club of 13 mining companies had never before owned a separated railroad. So while we could point to actual experience to answer questions about our future arrangements, the miners could not do likewise. There were no easy answers to basic questions like:

- Who would lead the consortium and how would shareholdings be divided?
- How would infrastructure priorities be decided?
- What if there was a disagreement between consortium members about the sequencing of investments?
- What would be the nature of the agreement between the ARTC and the consortium?
- How would the consortium treat small miners who were not part of the group, and new entrants to the Queensland mining industry?

- How would transition risks be managed given that the Queensland network has unique characteristics (for example narrow gauge, heavy haul, tropical environment, electrification)?

In addition to canvassing these matters in detail in our ACCC submission, we hammered these questions publicly and in conversations with State and Federal Government, industry players, suppliers, peak bodies and international contacts. A number of the meetings were vigorous and colourful, including one with the CEO of the Minerals Council of Australia Mitch Hooke. Doug Young and I met Hooke in Canberra at the height of the mining tax stoush with the Federal Government. Young began with a less than generous assessment of the behaviour of some mining companies in North America. And I thought we were going to be thrown out of the office when I described the QCIRG model as 'experimental', compared to our structure that had already delivered growth and competition in Queensland. But Hooke is a consummate professional, and I'm sure he saw the jousting as appropriate and understandable.

In late July 2010, we lodged our ACCC submission and followed up with a call, explaining that we were more than willing to provide further information face to face. Overall, there were 57 submissions, but these were never made public so we can only speculate about the groups that participated.

As indicated earlier, Jose Gomez Ibanez, a strong supporter of vertical integration, and the QR National float model, had expertly fielded questions at the ACCC's annual conference around the same time. Several Commissioners and senior Mergers and Acquisitions figures were in the audience.

We called the ACCC repeatedly to check progress on its review of the proposed QCIRG transaction, and reiterated our willingness to meet to expand on our main points. Our General Counsel David Wenck briefed leading competition lawyer Russell Miller, and we started planning a visit to Melbourne to take the Commission through the relevant issues as we saw them.

In August, the Commission surprised the mining lobby when it announced it was suspending the timeline for its review of the transaction, seeking further information from the coal companies. We didn't know exactly what this meant, but it looked like a good sign.

Matthew Stevens referred to the ACCC action as 'regulatory purgatory' for the miners.

'The intriguing thing about the delay is that no one involved imagined there would be too much concern at the regulatory level,' he wrote.[61]

Behind the scenes, though, this issue had been increasingly troubling the Treasurer of Queensland.

'The policy problem I had all along with it was that it was going to disadvantage smaller participants and provide an anti-competitive platform for new entrants,' Fraser says.

What was not a good sign was the increasing instability in the Queensland Labor Party. Government backbenchers were becoming worried about their prospects at the next State election, and began to think about leadership change. A large Queensland swing against Labor in the 21 August Federal Election was seen as a foretaste of what was to come in the 2012 State election.

Premier Bligh, however, stiffened her resolve. After many months of failing to connect with consistent key messages, she finally found a clear voice. Some likened her to the steely Margaret Thatcher.[62] Observers began to notice a clear contrast with previous Labor leaders, particularly in New South Wales, who had been swayed from their course on privatisation.

'I look over the border sometimes and wonder what might have been if (deposed Premier) Morris Iemma had been able to complete his asset sales,' Bligh told *The Australian*. 'No doubt, the anticipated $15 billion of revenue would have been put to good use. They would be possibly building the now-infamous Epping Rail line.'[63]

In the end, Premier Bligh stared down her detractors in a special Caucus meeting on 30 August 2010.

'I don't intend to let the NSW disease that sees leadership as a revolving door undermine a democratic mandate in Queensland,' Bligh told *The Courier Mail*.

'It hasn't worked in NSW and it failed miserably federally. Queensland will not be infected by the NSW corrosion.'[64]

Despite Premier Bligh dousing the flames of rebellion against her leadership, the QR National float decision was certainly in the balance.

'The government was under enormous political pressure,' Fraser says. 'We were in the middle of a hugely difficult program. Most of the opposition was external and to the left of us. They (the miners) thought that by applying pressure to the right they would contribute to the Government changing its mind.'

....

With the unions and the mining companies putting increasing pressure on the government, one of the major priorities for Hockridge and the rest of the team was to step up the direct engagement with employees. Ironically, the union's refusal to talk to the company helped our cause because management became, by default, the only credible source of up-to-date information about what was happening with the privatisation. The QR National team also had clear air to paint a picture of what a privatised railroad would look like. In late July and early September 2010, Hockridge and Corporate Affairs Manager Mark Hairsine covered tens of thousands of kilometres across Australia visiting and revisiting QR National's main work sites. During one three-day period in July, for example, Hockridge addressed more than 2,000 employees in the key Queensland locations of Brisbane, Ipswich, Townsville, Mackay, Rockhampton and Gladstone. Most meetings were in large open venues, to accommodate the sizeable crowds. There were some 400 people alone at one Redbank workshop meeting.

In orange 'hi-vis' overalls, Hockridge would start each town hall meeting with an impassioned defence of the IPO model and his vision of a private sector future for QR National. Hockridge assured the crowds that his intention was to grow the business, not pull it apart and drive it into the ground. Then he would open up to robust and often fiery question and answer sessions. While some audiences listened politely, others were less welcoming.

'Townsville was pretty ugly, with a group of employees in the crowd turning their backs on Lance during his entire address,' Hairsine says. 'Many people there thought that was pretty poor form.'

For the most part, though, employees listened respectfully. At each location, Hockridge fielded all the questions that people wanted answered, from queries about the privatisation process and shareholdings, through to personal enquiries about his salary and conditions. Hairsine says that while many remained unconvinced, they were happy to hear what he had to say.

'With some of the staff, you could see Lance was getting some traction and the mist was starting to lift,' Hairsine says. 'They were thinking, maybe this is going to work after all.'

··········

On the back of this direct work with employees, we stepped up our efforts to significantly differentiate ourselves from QCIRG. One of our important themes was that we were a long-term player committed to growth in employment and regional communities. We rejected the mining practice of fly-in, fly-out, preferring our people to live and work locally. And to drive our growth, we wanted to boost our apprentice intake, increase community sponsorships, and commit to more Indigenous employment. These themes were not cynically created in the heat of the battle – they were based on the strong beliefs of our own employees, communicated during an extensive two-month consultation process.

Member of the privatisation advisory team and former head of the Australian Industry Group Bob Herbert was a central player in developing this social and employment point of difference. With our approval, he developed a draft compact with unions, and socialised the idea with government and a number of federal union representatives. Although the unions were still not officially talking to us, the idea was seeded.

'The work with the unions helped to ameliorate the strength of their protests,' Herbert says. 'When they marched, they had very small crowds. It didn't quite hang together, a union movement working to unseat the government, and conspiring with the big end of town.'

John Stephens and Herbert also developed a skills plan to deal with the expected growth in our business in the coming years. We decided to publicly announce an increase in our intake for apprentices, graduates and trainees. Originally we had contemplated a doubling of our commitment, yet when we looked at the growth trends it was not going to be enough. In the end, we decided to triple our intake to 300 per year. This sent a very clear message that we were gearing up for major growth.

'It came late in the process but we were able to do something extraordinary to demonstrate our bona fides,' Herbert says. 'John Stephens was as solid as a rock through all of this. He was a really important player.'

Stephens agrees that we were able to make some progress behind the scenes with the more reasonable voices within the union movement.

'Some unions were less hostile, and more pragmatic,' he says. 'We had several good discussions with Andrew Dettmar, head of the AMWU and President of the ALP in Queensland. We were able to explain how we would position a privatised QRN, and what sort of a company we would be.'

Paul Cronin says most people could see the sincerity of what we were announcing.

'It's easy for people to be cynical about these announcements, but they were extensions of the kind of things QR had been doing for 140 years,' Cronin says.

In case anyone had missed the point, we launched a statewide advertising campaign to emphasise our new commitment to apprentices, and the idea of our people living and working locally.

Cronin then pulled off a public affairs masterstroke. A group of community leaders and business people from Central Queensland were busy putting together a bid for a new National Rugby League team based in Central Queensland. Because our network ran through the heart of this region, Cronin started courting the bid organisers and secured pole position for QRN as sponsor of the whole effort. It was hard to imagine a more powerful symbol of our commitment to these communities.

• • • • • • • • • • •

Despite this employee and community offensive, our position was looking shaky as the QCIRG battle entered its final phase in the first week of September 2010. We understood from media reports that if the government accepted the QCIRG bid, it would now consider keeping all above rail operations and the workshops in public hands. Premier Bligh was reported as actively considering such a structure. Then we became aware of a bombshell development. The unions had been in secret negotiations with the mining companies over what to do with employees if the mining bid succeeded.

'They were negotiating behind closed doors with the coal companies, and it would have resulted in job losses for some of their members,' Paul Cronin says. 'They needed to be upfront and transparent about it.'

A memo from Hockridge was sent to all QRN employees, alerting the workforce to the development, and urging them to 'contact your delegates to discover what, if anything has been discussed or agreed behind closed doors. These are decisions which affect your future, and you have a right to know.'

Hockridge also warned that keeping the 'above rail' operations and the workshops in government ownership would directly affect the viability of many jobs.

'I believe it will cost jobs and put at risk the very future of our company,' he said in the memo. 'If the above rail businesses were to be kept in public hands as suggested, I believe the business would slowly erode over time and the constraints of public ownership would once again limit any future growth.'

Unions were, of course, outraged by the memo and some people in Government wondered if QR National had lost the plot. The memo was immediately leaked to *The Australian*, which described it as 'blunt and bellicose'.[65] *The Australian Financial Review* labelled it 'bizarre'.[66]

'I had a few sleepless nights after putting it out, because of the strength of reaction from stakeholders,' Cronin says. 'But in the end it was about being open, honest and transparent with our employees.'

Interestingly, we understand that the Treasurer was not unhappy with our intervention.

'That was the low point – we suddenly had a coalition of the unwilling, circling around, from left to right,' Fraser recalls.

Fraser says that this move by the mining companies ratcheted up the pressure on the government, both inside and outside, to fix the 'political problem' that QR National had become.

'The options were pretty clear – to push ahead with the float, or abandon the transaction, and capitulate to the miners' campaign,' he says.

We continued with our last minute push to stress the advantages of a QRN IPO. In truth, we were fortunate that we had the ability to announce real decisions and investments, day after day. QCIRG only had a vague ideological model to point to.

In addition to our regional advertising campaign, we started a high profile tour of growth announcements. On 6 September, Hockridge visited areas involved in the $1.1 billion Northern Missing Link project that was to deliver up to 50 million tonnes of new capacity to the Queensland coal system. Two days later, he was in UGL's locomotive works in Sydney, drawing attention to the $145 million QRN was spending on 19 new locomotives for its Hunter Valley business. On 9 September, questioned by *The Australian Financial Review* on the miners' bid, Hockridge said: 'We're the pawn here, hopefully a very valuable one, and I can't honestly tell you exactly where it's at.'[67]

Every member of the team was trying to extract the last possible advantage from the days remaining before the government made its decision. We worked the phones furiously with potential supporters. I also asked a massive favour of Bob Herbert.

'Bob, we are in desperate straits,' I told him. 'Would you consider writing a letter to the editor of *The Courier Mail* on our behalf?'

Herbert wasn't sure that his voice would carry much weight but was more than happy to help. As a former head of the Australian Industry Group, I thought he was being overly modest.

On 7 September, I attended a lunch address by Premier Bligh at a function hosted by the Committee for Economic Development (CEDA). Inevitably, the QCIRG bid was included in her speech. Bligh re-iterated that the government was seriously considering the proposal. But I was surprised at her affirmation of the IPO alternative.

'QR National will be a top 50 ASX company,' she announced.

I was sitting next to Paul Scurrah, and he said, 'I think that's a tick for the IPO.'

Hockridge's view was still that it could go either way.

'In my view the Treasurer was solidly with us and had clearly nailed his colours to the mast, and repeatedly done so,' he says. 'But equally the pragmatist politician had to have regard to the financial and political reality.'

At around 5 pm on 9 September 2010, we were in a meeting on Level 14 of QRN headquarters in Edward Street. Hockridge walked into the meeting room, ashen-faced, and asked all people except members of the Executive Leadership Team, to leave.

'It indicated to me that we were gone,' Paul Cronin said. I admit I had the same view.

But to our delight, it was the opposite outcome. 'I have just been informed that QCIRG has withdrawn its bid for the coal network,' Hockridge told us.

He insists now that he was not being deliberately manipulative with our emotions.

'Given the importance of what had happened, it was critically important that what I was about to say was not transmitted widely,' he says. 'For myself, it hadn't quite sunk in. I wasn't feeling jubilant. I was thinking about the mountain of stuff that we had to do.'

In the immediate aftermath of the QCIRG announcement, Hockridge told managers to focus on the job at hand, and stay professional, and under no circumstances was there to be hubris or gloating. There were grave, controlled nods around the table.

On the inside, we were all doing cartwheels, but managed to maintain our serious faces for at least a few minutes. David Wenck and I stepped into the lift after the meeting. Wenck turned to me and said, 'What about some gloating?' and we then celebrated in proper fashion!

The first people I called were Terry Cutler and Bob Herbert, who had been such influential members of our internal strategy team. Both of course were cock-a-hoop. The next morning Bob Herbert's letter appeared in *The Courier Mail*. It seemed a little out of context, given that the QCIRG bid had collapsed. But many of its sentiments still rang true.

'The Queensland Government made the correct decision to proceed almost a year ago,' Herbert wrote. 'The worst move it could now make is to backtrack for no good cause – certainly not because it is spooked by recent political outcomes or the hankerings of unions whose members, QR National employees, are voluntarily engaging with the new enterprise.'

'Queenslanders want certainty from their leadership, built around a vision for the future. Now is the time for the government to be true to its convictions.'[68]

· · · · · · · · · · · ·

And sure enough, Premier Bligh and Treasurer Fraser pressed on resolutely, announcing on 12 October that QR National would float on 22 November 2010. But perhaps relieved at negotiating the hurdle of the miners' bid, Bligh allowed herself a bit of light-hearted banter at the official float launch, musing that few would see the IPO document as a 'bodice-ripper'. Tim Boreham at *The Australian* concurred. 'As far as potboilers go, D. H. Lawrence can relax.'[69]

There were the inevitable recriminations within the mining camp. It turned out that just two days before QCIRG was due to lodge its formal, binding offer, Anglo American dramatically reduced its equity contribution. Instead of its original $460 million commitment, it told its consortium partners it could only manage $35 million, because its investment committee could not justify the original amount. *The Australian* reported that Anglo's chief concern had been the Queensland Government's insistence that QCIRG accept all regulatory risk. With the ACCC yet to clear the deal, that was a major uncertainty.[70]

The view from within the consortium was that finding common interest was difficult.

'It wasn't efficient – you had half a dozen mining companies, all with different approaches,' recalls former Macarthur Coal Chair Keith De Lacy. 'So it was fraught with its own problems. When you've got to get a consensus and you get into a competitive bidding war, it's very difficult. Some people are more risk-takers than others.'

'I thought despite this that the consortium would be successful. But I think I underestimated the commercial capability of the QR team. And that's probably a bit to do with 50 years of knowing QR, and never having had to ever be in a competitive, hard-nosed environment with them. I take my hat off to them.'

During the exhausting battle with the mining companies, Treasurer Fraser was pilloried for labelling their bid as a 'stunt'. But in the end, he was vindicated. As he saw it, what divided the companies was stronger than what united them. Their overriding priority was competition with each other, not the ownership of rail infrastructure in Queensland.

'The notion that they were ever going to be able to hold all of this in a way that provided for their divergent interests to be converged, seemed to me to be implausible,' he says. 'And ultimately it was.'

In the end, Fraser believed that the mining companies were motivated by a desire to preserve a government-owned QR.

'Under that structure, they knew that whatever happened at a commercial level, they could always seek to overturn by applying political pressure,' Fraser says. 'It was always in their interests to have the capital of the taxpayer tied up, not necessarily with the most efficient timing. They didn't mind the taxpayers' capital being applied inefficiently because it was something that didn't concern their own balance sheets.'

············

We will never know, of course, what the government would have done if QCIRG had managed to agree on a formal bid. According to Hockridge, an integrated float may still have been the outcome.

'Even if a bid had eventuated, we would still have been in with a chance,' he says. 'What would you have done with the above rail? Would you have seriously kept it together? Would they have sold for whatever they could get? Would they have sold the interstate operations and kept Queensland? The industrial relations difficulty with all of these options was evident.'

With the mining bid dead, the QR National team turned its attention to executing the second biggest government float in Australia's history.

CHAPTER FOURTEEN

Leaving the station

W hile the privatisation team had been fighting for the company's survival, hundreds of QR National employees had been quietly working on the thousands of steps necessary for QR National to float in November of 2010.

At times, it would have been difficult for these dedicated people to keep their minds on the job, because much of what they were reading in daily media was suggesting it may all be in vain.

Despite the churning emotions, and sleepless nights, the QR National IPO task force demonstrated a methodical, relentless professionalism that impressed a number of outsiders, including the Treasurer himself.

'Regardless of the policy issues, the execution of it was a first class effort,' Fraser says.

At the start of the process, there was a strong view outside that QR National and the government did not have the ability or the time to get ready for a float by November 2010.

'I can't tell you how many people, including QR's major competitor, pulled me aside and said, "By the way, if you think you can get this thing floated by the end of 2010 you are smoking dope",' Matt Keenan recalls.

As we have seen, Brendon Gibson led the group that firstly completed the separation from Queensland Rail, and then prepared QR National for listing. We knew what we owned and who we employed, but we were nowhere near ready for the intense scrutiny that would surely follow from bankers, auditors and ultimately potential investors.

Gibson, Colin Keel and Darren Barlow were the key drivers, and fixers, relying on scores of people within the business units to complete the detail. Hundreds of thousands of pages of documentation were produced, thousands of questions were answered, and every day involved a sticking point which required yet another agreement with the government.

O'Toole took the reins of this challenge, sorting out many stalemates face to face with the head of the Treasury transaction team, Tim Spencer. O'Toole remembers one key meeting when both of them laid their cards on the table. She acknowledged to Spencer that despite her private sector experience, she had never executed a privatisation, and certainly nothing on this scale. Spencer shared that although he had run trade sale processes before, he had never steered a listed privatisation.

'We agreed that we were absolutely doomed if we didn't work together and share,' O'Toole recalls.

On a number of occasions during the float process, O'Toole and Spencer would reach stalemate. They would need to excuse themselves from a room full of advisors, and talk things through quietly one to one. O'Toole believes that she and Spencer established not so much a trusting relationship, but one that was pragmatic and respectful one on both sides.

While O'Toole and Spencer were putting out bushfires daily, Prescott and Hockridge stayed involved in the strategic decisions. There was a weekly meeting involving Prescott, Hockridge, Spencer and Spencer's boss, Under Treasurer Gerard Bradley.

Some dilemmas called for creativity, rather than methodical execution. As we have seen, the Premier announced early on that the North Coast Line (NCL), which connects Brisbane to regional Queensland capitals, would remain in government hands. This sounded fine at first blush, except that from Gladstone to Rockhampton the NCL had connections with the QR National coal network. QR National was in danger of not having control of its railroad all the way through to the port.

Gibson's team worked hard to have the relevant section of the North Coast Line included in QR National's lease. The government was resolute – that would simply not be allowed. After much handwringing and pleading, Gibson devised an elegant compromise that gave both sides what they needed. The key part of the North Coast Line would remain in government hands, and not be part of the QRN lease, but its operational control would rest with QRN.

This issue, along with many others, required expert input from the Network business. The long-suffering Executive General Manager Network Mike Carter had also been a key player in developing the integrated privatisation model. He was also involved in the direct tussle with the QCIRG bidders. And while everyone else moved on to other things when the miners pulled out, Carter was not able to avoid them.

On 14 September 2010, Carter was boosted by the news that the National Competition Council had released a draft recommendation that the Central Queensland coal network not be placed under federal control. It announced a further draft recommendation that the Queensland Rail Access Regime be certified as effective for a period of 10 years. This followed detailed submissions from QR National and the Queensland Government.

However, Carter's team had literally just a few weeks to negotiate the pricing principles and access rules that would govern the operation of the network that would be owned by a privatised QR National. As Carter saw it, once the mining companies had failed in their QCIRG bid, they were able to devote resources to 'tying QR National up in knots' over the access undertaking.

'As the line executive in the fray that was very challenging,' Carter says. 'That period was quite intensive because we were pushed right up against the deadlines for getting the share offer document out. There was a strong desire to have the regulatory arrangement bedded down because otherwise there would be no certainty for arguably the organisation's largest cash-flow.'

Carter says if agreement had not been reached, it could have derailed the float or at the least, had a material effect.

'It went right down to the wire, with Queensland Competition Authority (QCA) meetings on weekends,' he says. 'We were negotiating with both hands tied behind our backs, both feet nailed to the floor and only allowed to speak when we were spoken to. But somehow we managed to find a way through.'

On 1 October, to the relief of Carter and the entire privatisation team, the QCA approved QR Network's third access undertaking (UT3).

Carter was involved in so much during this ultimate year of change. He looks back on it now with some satisfaction.

'It was the hardest year of my working life without a doubt,' Carter says. 'I had the challenge of the float, the separation, the undertaking and the miners' bid. But I wouldn't swap it for anything. And to the team that was with me, they kept it all going, with me missing in action for most of the year.'

While this battle was going on, others were tackling more symbolic issues. The IPO team made a major effort during this period to make another bold break with the past, and change the QR National name. No one could argue that there wasn't confusion between our company and the railway that remained government-owned, Queensland Rail. Even Premier Bligh on occasion got the two companies mixed up. We thought that a new name would also help us to mark the change in the eyes of our people and our customers.

Lindsay Woodland, at the time QR National's head of Investor Relations, had been through a thorough process to devise and market test a new branding. Premier Bligh and Treasurer Fraser were happy with the new branding (logo and colours) but baulked at the new name. We understood that Treasurer Fraser was particularly insistent on this matter, arguing that the Q had not been a barrier to the national and international growth of Qantas, which of course started life as the Queensland and Northern Territory Aerial Service.

With the big decisions made, and most information sources in place, Treasury, QR National and the banks advising the government on the float set about putting together the offer document and supporting material. I realised first-hand how difficult this must have been, because in early 2010 I had compiled a very brief summary of the company that was used by John Prescott to brief potential directors. The lawyers had struck out most of my draft!

The exhaustive legal requirements of a public offer meant there were minefields everywhere. And the problems were compounded by the global nature of our float. For example, the IPO rules in the USA differ in key respects from those in Australia, and so other than the offer document being provided to institutional investors, our documents were not legally permitted to be seen in that country. These publications needed to carry a special disclaimer.

Colin Keel was the project manager for the compilation and printing of the offer document. There were scores of drafts, which were circulated to managers and technical experts for progressive input. It was a painstaking process, where facts had to be gathered, then checked and rechecked with the business units. There were thousands of questions to deal with from bankers and auditors.

The drafters, on the whole, did a phenomenal job, although some embarrassments were only corrected late in the piece. For example, I noticed in the Industry Overview section that South Australia did not appear to have a railroad. It is admittedly small by Queensland standards, but it definitely exists!

Because at the time the mining companies' bid was still live, we had to keep pushing back crucial print deadlines. As we entered September 2010, there had still been no definitive answer on the bid, and yet the potential float was only two months away. Keel, in consultation with Hockridge, O'Toole and the State, decided we would need to start printing regardless. For a week or so, we lived with the embarrassing possibility of needing to shred 500,000 glossy 150-page offer documents.

CHAPTER FIFTEEN

Going to market

The QR National float came to the market during a difficult time. The overhang from the global financial crisis was still tangible, exemplified by the very patchy post-crisis IPO record in Australia. The largest and highest profile float of recent times had been the uninspiring Australian retail giant Myer, offloaded by private equity firm Texas Pacific Group (TPG). After floating in November 2009 at $4.10, and despite the eye-catching sponsorship of former Miss Universe Jennifer Hawkins, Myer shares quickly lost nearly half of their issue value.

Up to the QRN float in November, there had been around 50 ASX floats of various sizes in 2010. More than half were languishing below their issue prices. But there were some quality first-timers bucking the trend. The second largest float of the year, the $1.2 billion Aston Resources IPO, had performed well. Bankers at the heart of the QR National transaction, like CBA's Leon

Allen, were noting however that Aston was seen as an exception to the overall gloomy IPO mood.

'Some fairly hard and fast positions were taken,' Allen says. 'The negativity of the GFC led many to think, 'hang on, they've pushed this on to the market early – I'm not going to be a participant in something that's not going to work.'

'They were sitting there thinking, "Am I going to suck up my time and money into this stock now or do I just sit there and wait for it to suffer the same fate of the other IPOs?"'

As Allen saw it, and many agreed with him, the private equity-led IPOs at the time, such as the disappointing Myer Holdings debut, had made Australian investors extremely wary.

What many in Australia were missing was the relatively sanguine reception for floats overseas, particularly in Asia. Dozens of significant IPOs were listed successfully in Asia in the latter half of 2010, including the $3.07 billion float of Singapore's Global Logistics Properties and a $1.1 billion listing for China's Ningbo Port.

The government had brought in investment banking's biggest guns to steer the float. In July 2010, it appointed five banks as joint lead managers (JLMs) – Credit Suisse, Goldman Sachs, Merrill Lynch, RBS Morgans and UBS. Appointed as co-lead managers were the CBA (represented by Leon Allen) and Brisbane-based Wilson HTM.

They certainly had their hands full as the QRN float entered its crucial final months. On top of a general disquiet over Australian floats, specific questions were being raised about the strength of the QRN business and its prospects. With QRN already one of the highest profile business stories because of the Government's tussle with the miners and the unions, we became daily fare in the financial media with increasing doubts about our forecasts and float narrative. The QRN price-earnings ratio (21 to 25 times projected FY11 earnings) was based on an assessment of the company's expected revenue and earnings growth. To many high-profile, self-appointed commentators, including Lindsay Fox, the head of the Australian trucking company, Linfox, it was unrealistically high.

Fox told a business lunch in Brisbane that he doubted that QR National's management would be able to resolve workforce issues and meet the growth forecasts in the offer document sent to investors. He seemed to cast doubt not only on the QR National float, but virtually every public offering process.

'I have never seen the acquisition of a company where in the first three to four years, the objectives have been achieved which were part of the prospectus,' *The Australian Financial Review* reported him as saying.

'If somebody offered me those multiples I would float my company,' he said. 'That is a hell of a multiple.'[71]

Critics were also unimpressed by the dividend yield, which was less than three per cent. This was seen by many as a major disincentive for 'Mum and Dad' retail investors. However, it was a very clear part of the overall message – QRN was being packaged as a low dividend, high growth play. As the Treasurer Andrew Fraser put it regularly 'If you are thinking about your grandchildren's education, this is the kind of stock that you put in a portfolio.'[72]

'I was surprised at the resistance, indeed the outright opposition,' says Hockridge. 'Ultimately everybody has the right to exercise their own judgment, but what concerned me were the people who were prepared to make observations that were clearly wrong when you looked at the facts.'

CBA's Leon Allen says the story was much more news-friendly as a tale of negativity.

'There's more to be gained from a story that has the government botching the biggest float in decades,' Allen says. 'Then that view gets reinforced and before you know it the sentiment is "oh yeah I can see what's wrong with it", rather than "let's have a look at this in an optimistic sense." And that whole negative cycle kept playing out week after week.'

Allen also says that the QRN brand suffered from a lack of visibility, particularly in States outside Queensland.

'It was very much a Queensland story despite the Australian dimension to it with the operations in NSW and Western Australia,' he says. 'It wasn't Telstra, where recognition was easy because there was a phone in every home. This instead was railing coal from Central Queensland to the Coast, and that's a big drive for your average Sydney funds manager.'

A narrative began to develop in Australia that Hockridge and his team were simply not up to the job. An anonymous analyst told Jenny Wiggins from *The Australian Financial Review* that while Hockridge was a good operations manager, 'the key issue is he hasn't run a public entity on his own before.'[73] Questions were being asked about his ability to turn customer relationships around, as well as his ability to communicate with investors.

More anonymous experts warmed to the theme. 'QR has been so badly run for so long it's hard to get excited about it being run better,' one deep thinker postulated.[74] An unnamed fund manager called for changes to the management structure. 'These guys are worse than Telstra. They do not have as a central motivation the customer.'[75]

Very few were taking a step back and considering the float in a historical context. If they had done so, they would have noticed a pretty fair track record for the IPO privatisations of large government organisations. There was strong evidence of major turnaround at North American rail privatisations like Canadian National and Conrail. And in Australia, while there had been no rail IPOs, most of the government floats had been successful for investors. *The Australian Financial Review* assessed a collection of these transactions, including Qantas, Telstra and the Commonwealth Bank, and found that the average share price lift in the first year of trading was 35 per cent.[76]

But many did not see the same potential in QR National. Ian Verrender, business reporter with the *Sydney Morning Herald*, was scathing.

'There's a golden rule when investing in floats, or IPOs,' wrote Verrender. 'Avoid floats where the owner is bailing out. Look for opportunities where an owner is hanging in and looking to fund an expansion. Anna Bligh is bailing.'[77]

And BBY analyst Moira Daw said 'We do not like an organisation that has to achieve a fundamental change in its culture.'[78]

One expert seemed to completely miss the point of government privatisations, and political reality, when they mused: 'Perhaps they should wait a few more years before they bring this to market.'[79]

In the face of this unremitting negativity, the IPO team, the Queensland Government, and the investment banks realised that they needed a circuit breaker. Impressed by the Hockridge and O'Toole re-telling of the CN privatisation story, some of the bankers wondered if North American investors in particular may warm to an antipodean railroad opportunity that bore many of the same hallmarks. Plans started being hatched to test this theory first-hand as early as possible.

. . . .

In the meantime, the company pressed ahead with a core building block for any top 50 listed company – the identification and recruitment of a high-calibre board of directors. John Prescott was well aware that board quality had been a key ingredient in the success of the 1995 CN privatisation.

The QRN process was of course complicated by the involvement of government, but it ran reasonably smoothly. Prescott decided on the combination of skills and competence the company would need, discussed this criteria with government, and then approached people that he knew would have the right mix.

'We also looked for a great degree of gender balance and while I would have preferred to have more women, we did make approaches to others who simply were too busy,' Prescott says.

The board was balanced, diverse and capable. QRN had secured the services of Shell Australia Chair Russell Caplan, former Pacific National director Allan Davies, former Australia Post CEO Graeme John, former Wesfarmers director Gene Tilbrook, former ARTC director and Australian Airlines chief executive Andrea Staines, and former managing partner at Blake Dawson, John Atkin. The board was also strengthened by the presence of the ex-head of the agricultural industry peak body Agforce Peter Kenny, who sadly passed away in 2011. Lance Hockridge was Managing Director and CEO, with John Prescott remaining as Chair.

'At the time, my thought was that we've got people with real financial management and capital raising skill,' Prescott says. 'We've got people with a clear appreciation of how large, operational businesses should be managed. We've got people with an understanding of the regulatory environment in which we operate. We've got people with appropriate industrial relations competencies, who would bring a civil and balanced approach.'

Prescott says the focus was on people who were directors, CEOs or senior advisors with top 50 companies because 'that's where we expected to end up'.

'I think the makeup of the board was absolutely crucial to the float,' he says. 'That's in respect of the contributions directors have made, the confidence they were able to generate from government, the guidance given to the management team, and in their preparedness to allow management to get on with things. I was confident they would be well received by the investment community and they have been.'

Even QRN's harshest critic, Matthew Stevens, still at *The Australian*, gave Prescott a bouquet for the calibre of the board.

'Putting aside the privatisation debate, it has to be acknowledged that Prescott has done a fair old job of assembling a board to run QR into the future,' Stevens wrote.

'Each in their own way adds credibility to the QR cause, although probably none more than one of the incumbents who has accepted Prescott's invitation to stay around after the IPO, Allan Davies. Davies has serious coal cred with long experience as a mine operator and rail services provider in the Hunter Valley.'[80]

CHAPTER SIXTEEN

Hitting the road

There's a concept in Australia known as the cultural cringe. Stemming from the days when we were just a colonial outpost of the UK, it describes a view that any Australian cultural output, from art to music, is inferior to what can be produced by the Brits, the Americans or the Europeans.

The QR National team never had a cultural cringe about the quality of its assets, its people, or the long-term opportunity the whole combination represented. We knew we had something unique, powerful, and worth fighting for. Something of global significance.

So when some of the bankers suggested to Hockridge and O'Toole that in light of lukewarm Australian sentiment we test the appetite of international investors, it became a priority. Given the accelerated timeframe of the float, however, there was no time to lose.

Despite its quality, QR National was completely unknown to global investors. The bankers advised that it was unrealistic to expect that people would be able to get their heads around the complicated story in one sitting. There would need to be several stages with each investor to build the compelling case, develop deep individual relationships, and finally win investment commitments worth hundreds of millions of dollars.

Hockridge and O'Toole had already made management changes so that they could focus their entire attention on the privatisation and IPO. Ken Lewsey had been appointed Acting CEO and Martin Moore had taken the reins as Acting CFO. Hockridge and O'Toole now realised that in addition to managing the myriad domestic challenges of the IPO, they would also need to spend a great deal of mid and late 2010 on the road. It was to be a gruelling, at times frustrating but ultimately incredibly rewarding experience.

In a pivotal move, from May to July 2010, QR National ran, in two phases, a pre-marketing roadshow in North America, Europe and Asia. Accompanied by different investment banks in each region, Hockridge and O'Toole introduced themselves and seeded the float idea with scores of potential investors in an intense couple of weeks.

For the first New York pre-marketing roadshow, they were joined by two key advisors from Credit Suisse, Prue Mackenzie (who would later join QR/ Aurizon) and Ian Buckley. Mackenzie remembers that the reaction from the Americans was unbelievable.

'It was of course still unproven, but the US guys just absolutely loved it,' Mackenzie says. 'They understood the vertical integration, they understood the transformation opportunity. Just before I boarded the plane back to Australia, I sent the rest of the team an email to say that the level of support here could be a game-changer.'

Hockridge also sensed early that international investors were intrigued, but knew that layers needed to be built over several visits.

'These first meetings were extremely important in that by the time we came back on the official roadshow we were talking about the value proposition rather than QRN 101,' he says.

International investors had a completely different frame of reference. Outside Australia, railroading is largely seen as a reliable and profitable investment category. Listed Class 1 North American railroads in particular had delivered consistently for investors over many years.

International investors were also taking comfort from QRN's Australian location, seeing it as a secure investment destination, with stable markets and low political risk. And rather than following the daily controversies about QRN in the Australian media, international investors quietly and dispassionately investigated the company's assets, pricing, management, customers and markets. With nearly half of the QRN business focussed on coal, investors needed to get comfortable about the sustainability of the Indian and Chinese demand for coal, and the security of Australian coal mines on the cost curve.

'It was not just the level of interest overseas, it was the nature of the interest,' Hockridge says. 'People could see the context of privatisation and its upside potential, the context of railroads, and how this organisation fitted with the Class 1s. Plus the extent of the exposure to the resource sector in Australia. It was a very, very different reaction.'

The European leg of the pre-marketing roadshow included a London meeting with the Children's Investment Fund (TCI), which had been founded by Chris Hohn in 2003. TCI launched a meticulous and detailed process to assess the QRN opportunity.

Oscar Hattink, who was at the time running TCI's global transport portfolio, saw parallels between QRN's business and the largest coal basin in the USA, the Powder River Basin.

'The economics favour the transporters. I saw good potential for an improvement in return on capital for QRN, provided the service was there,' Hattink says.

To understand the potential for improving service and growing the business, Hattink spoke to most of the players. He spent time with Hockridge, O'Toole, and the Queensland Government, and gained further confidence in the company's future.

'It became clear this was a long term story that could fit with my portfolio,' he says.

Having planted a seed with potential international investors, planning began on a five-week official global roadshow in September and October 2010. When the Queensland Government first suggested to O'Toole that a professional media logistics firm manage the roadshow, she couldn't see the point. After all, she argued, hadn't QR National just successfully navigated their way around the pre-marketing roadshow?

But nothing could have prepared the team for the gruelling nature of the real thing. In five weeks, the IPO team travelled to four continents, held 171 formal meetings with investors, and interacted face to face with more than 2,000 potential prospects. Lindsay Woodland, QRN's Senior Vice President Investor Relations, recalls the unrelenting schedule.

Each day would be a marathon. Up every morning before 6 am to prepare for the day, and check understanding of the companies and the people you were going to see. Eight one-hour meetings per day with individual investors. Breakfast meetings, brunch meetings, coffee meetings, meetings in the car if necessary. Last formal meeting at 7 pm. Conference call in the car on the way back to the hotel. Fly to another city that night, or review the day over dinner and think about the next day. Then do it all the next day. Seven days a week.

Faced by this prospect when the roadshow was in the final stages of planning, O'Toole gave way and professional help was sought. London-based Media Tree was commissioned to manage the roadshow logistics, with CEO Jamie Griffiths the key man on the ground for the QRN project. Media Tree had global experience, having handled many of the world telecommunications floats, including Telstra. Griffiths' team would play every role from communications consultants to executive nannies.

As Griffiths sees it, the key was to ensure that clients did not have to think of anything logistical. Waking up, transport, luggage, checking out, documentation, timetables. Especially timetables.

'Even if you're having a good meeting and you want to talk to the investor further, I'm there to say you can't,' he says.

Media Tree ran the schedule from a Roadshow Desk at their London headquarters, where they would liaise with banks 24 hours a day to ensure that every element of the logistics for each meeting was carefully managed.

While the 'one-on-one' meetings were the most common, in cities like Sydney, London, Hong Kong and New York where it was impossible to see every potential investor individually, large meetings were held to brief up to

100 investors at a time. For these events, Media Tree would send an advance team in a day before to set up backdrops, test the staging, lighting, and sound, and check for last-minute gremlins.

Media Tree had dealt before with difficult bankers, hotel booking disasters, and ash-clouds that destroyed air travel schedules. In the QRN case, while there were no weather-related catastrophes, there were some unexpected obstacles early on, courtesy of the Queensland Government.

Media Tree has a specifically designed staging bespoke to roadshows. It is lightweight, effective and versatile, and has been used around the world. But the government had a different plan.

'The government didn't believe me, and they went off all around Australia to try to find someone else to build all this staging,' Griffiths says. 'They eventually came back to me with their tail between their legs, and said, 'Oh yes, your system does seem to be much more cost effective.''

The roadshow kick-off was also not helped by a safety issue on the first day. If Media Tree and the JLMs were in any doubt about Lance Hockridge's commitment to safety, that disappeared quickly.

'I absolutely spat the dummy because the driver we had was doing things in Melbourne that were borderline safety-wise,' Hockridge says. 'At one point, he did a U-turn on Collins Street and the traffic closed him up on the side and so he was straddling the tram lines with nowhere to go. He received the benefit of my view about that behaviour and what my expectations were thereafter.'

The fraught atmosphere of the first week of the roadshow in Australia was not helped by the lukewarm investor reaction to the QRN presentations. The daily diet of negativity about QRN in the financial media set the tone, and many prospects were sceptical and cynical.

Having never seen a railroad float locally, these investors found it difficult to contextualise what they were seeing. Most compared the QRN prospect erroneously with its coal haulage competitor Asciano. Asciano is not a 'pure play' railroad stock, because half of its company is devoted to port operations. Even its rail business is not comparable because it owns no 'below rail' railway infrastructure.

Other Australian investors unfamiliar with listed railroads opined about their greater comfort with 'direct' investment in commodities coal through major mining companies. Yet on any analysis, the major mining companies were actually less leveraged to coal than QRN.

On the last day of the Australian leg of the roadshow, *The Australian Financial Review* summed up the mood in a story headlined 'Less than compelling offer'. Clime Investment Management Chief Investment Officer John Abernethy was blunt.

'You would have to have rocks in your head to say this is a compelling buy compared to what else is out there in the market,' he said, adding, 'We value the business at less than its equity and suggest long term investors give this float the wide berth.'[81]

Elsewhere in the story, the problems and risks identified by 'value' investors included 'loss of market share in Queensland, reduced demand for export coal, high levels of capital expenditure, and adverse weather, such as earthquakes or floods.' Apart from that, the float was clearly a slam dunk!

············

Ultimately, the team was pleased to leave Australian shores and seek better fortune in Asia, Europe and finally North America. The false start in Australia made the task clear but daunting.

One lunch in New York, attended by about 80 potential investors, was a particular highlight. Woodland recalls that Hockridge and O'Toole were particularly 'on form'.

'There was this feeling in the room of anticipation and excitement,' Woodland says. 'Afterwards, it was almost like a mobbing. These investors raced up to the stage to talk to Lance and Deb privately, and there were questions for another half an hour. The level of excitement was clear – it was just electric.'

This New York lunch was viewed as a real turning point in the roadshow. Leading fund Scout Capital was there, liked what they saw and requested a follow up. Ultimately Scout would become one of the QR National's largest shareholders.

Scout would not only decide to invest heavily in the stock but also told their peers about QRN. In an article in a hedge fund industry newsletter, Scout spoke expansively about the company and how impressed they were.

Woodland was struck by the vastly different approach of the North American investors. For example, these investors focussed on the price to book ratio. With North America railroads it was around two, whereas QRN's ratio was closer to one at the time. Long-term outlook was also key, and again the comparisons with North America were favourable. Privatisations like CN and Conrail had delivered impressive long-term turnarounds, and American investors could see no reason why QRN would not be the same.

However, while investors were interested, and some excited, converting this into cheque-book action was a tough process. Woodland believes that management capability was one of the most important factors in closing the deal with many. The toughest and brightest investment representatives in the world put Hockridge under intense scrutiny.

'There were a couple of times there where it was like Lance was being interviewed for a job, and I guess in a way, he was,' Woodland says. 'He was well and truly grilled about his background, his experience, and what the company could achieve.'

With this degree of intensity during the five week roadshow, there was little opportunity for levity or relaxation. But Griffiths hatched a plan to help the group at least let off a little steam.

'At the end of the day, we would always try to get out for some proper food, and try to relax,' Griffiths says. 'I needed to make sure we went to places that they would enjoy.'

This turned into a keenly fought contest, in which every team member proposed at least one venue. At the end of the trip, the group was asked to rank the choices. O'Toole's choice was memorable, but for all the wrong reasons.

'Deb chose somewhere in London that she and her husband had been to, that was supposedly amazing, but it ended up being a total disaster,' says Griffiths.

Hockridge was even more damming.

'It was a Chinese restaurant, Mr Choo's or something,' he says. 'Deb had raved about it, but we turned up and it was a hovel. They sat eleven of us around a table designed for about six.'

Griffiths looked to rescue the situation with his next choice – a pub meal in the English countryside.

'I took them one Saturday to Winchester. We saw the Cathedral, and relaxed in the pub for a big meal with a few beers. That choice ended up coming second in the global competition, which wasn't bad. I told the publican later and he was really chuffed.'

As the roadshow rolled on, the spirit in the group was obviously buoyed by the increasingly positive reactions from investors. There were many factors in this building momentum, but a key ingredient was the insight and hard work of many of the investment bankers. The banks, themselves captivated by this unusual but very attractive float, had lined up hundreds of meetings, given exhaustive background to investors and furiously worked the phones with media.

The understandable fatigue from five weeks on the road, not to mention the previous pre-marketing roadtrips, was not affecting energy levels, or performance at meetings and events. The roadshow troupe had a collective sense that support was building, and that investment history was being made.

There was always, however, a negative media call from Australia to bring the group back to reality. Towards the end of the roadshow, Merrill Lynch's Guy Foster took a call in the car from a journalist with *The Australian Financial Review*. The rest of the group listened as Foster's voice grew louder while he remonstrated with the reporter. Foster ended the call by theatrically declaring the journalist would 'eternally regret' getting this so badly wrong. It provided much-needed light relief to the travel-weary team.

The result of all of this international activity was nothing short of remarkable. Investors in North America and Europe in particular were captivated. TCI for example, was contemplating QR National as one of their key long-term investments. In the last few weeks before the float, Matt Keenan and TCI's Oscar Hattink were in ongoing contact. Keenan recalls that in one phone hook-up Oscar complained about time zones and having to take calls in the early morning.

'I said, well why don't you fly over here and we can chat while we surf?' Keenan recalls.

Hattink, a very keen surfer, was intrigued.

'Every year I go surfing,' he says. 'I was tossing up whether to go to Omaha, but it was very cold. So I decided I would hop on a plane and take Matt up on the offer. I flew to Sydney for a couple of days. On the morning before the bookbuild opened, Matt and about ten other guys took me out to Bondi, and we were surfing and talking. I like to do deals in the sea, but this was the first on a surfboard!'

············

TCI's bid into the book was one of the first received, and the company would emerge as the largest initial shareholder in QRN (excluding the residual shareholding of the Queensland Government). New York-based Scout Capital also invested heavily, part of a North American contingent which made up around 30 per cent of the share register. Out of hundreds of meetings, a small group of quality funds were compelled by the story and were determined to become foundation owners. Because the domestic institutions had largely vacated the field, they had greater potential to take more substantial positions, although the 15 per cent cap on single ownership stopped greater ambitions from taking hold.

Leon Allen says the overseas funds had simpler, clearer criteria on which to judge the stock. Spectacularly successful Class 1 railroads like CN and BNSF, readily identified as possible examples of QRN's future, made the job a whole lot easier.

'You could walk in there and say guess what, we're hinged to China, we have this network, we have above rail with a good position, we have capability, assets and investments,' Allen says. 'And we're going to be privatised and here are the people that are going to run the company. He's from Bluescope North America, he's from BHP. And they've just gone tick tick tick tick tick. We get it, we're willing to buy the growth story.'

Lance Hockridge is sure that international investors saved the float.

'There is a lesson here for future IPOs,' he says. 'We had the privatisation upside, the direct points of comparison, and our leverage to the resources sector. But the other thing we had was scope and scale. If this had been a somewhat smaller IPO we wouldn't have needed the offshore support. On the other hand, we wouldn't have got the support if we'd been smaller.'

Even critics of QRN were forced to acknowledge the extent of the work being done by overseas investors. As then Asciano CEO Mark Rowsthorn told

The Australian Financial Review shortly after the QRN float: 'The extent of their due diligence (on QR National) was amazing ... either they're very right or very wrong.'[02]

CHAPTER SEVENTEEN

Black bookbuild

There is an episode of the manic British comedy *Black Books* in which an innocent customer walks into Bernard's bizarre bookshop and asks, perfectly reasonably, whether the store has a particular title. Bernard snaps, 'How would I know? Go to a proper bookshop.'

In the weeks before a public float, the vendor and potential institutional buyers go into an elaborate mating dance, known as a bookbuild. In the case of QR National, this followed a long process of courting retail shareholders (Mums and Dads), which had been reasonably successful, accounting for roughly $1 billion of the total sale. Institutions were now being asked to bid for allocations within the price range that had been set by the government of $2.50 to $3.00 per share.

The QRN bookbuild was sprinkled with high comedy and drama, with each delicious twist played out in full public view via the financial media. In the end, domestic institutions treated the bookbuild process with so much contempt that you could have been forgiven for thinking Bernard the bookshop owner was in charge.

Lance Hockridge and Deb O'Toole had returned to Australia in mid-November 2010 buoyed by the overseas reaction, but still unclear about whether that interest would be converted into bankable support. Hit again by the cold reality of domestic scepticism, it was natural for Hockridge to wonder if the promise of those strong handshakes in New York and London would prove illusory.

QRN was without doubt the biggest financial story of the year, which led to something of a feeding frenzy. Even before the soap opera of the bookbuild, scribes were digging for any half-decent angle on the story. As we have seen, space was found for concerns about QRN losing future market share in Queensland (the company had already acknowledged this as inevitable). Asciano complaints about QRN's approach to track access and pricing made the cut. And according to some observers, climate change loomed as a killer for the float.

The Age's Paddy Manning wrote:

'In 2007, NASA climate scientists likened coal trains to "death trains – no less gruesome than if they were boxcars headed to crematoriums, loaded with uncountable irreplaceable species." Emotive perhaps but you can understand why QR National chief executive Lance Hockridge shied away from an interview about climate change this week.'[83]

In the millions of column inches devoted to the QRN yarn during 2010, however, it is clear that there were two very carefully organised media 'campaigns' against our plans. The first was led by Nick Greiner and the QCIRG mining consortium. The second involved domestic institutional investors in the lead-up to the bookbuild.

Domestic institutions were highly sceptical about the QRN float from the outset. But because of its size, it could not be ignored. They saw a seemingly boyish Treasurer wrestling with a massive transaction, and a management team that seemed continually in crisis mode – first fighting for the right structure, then fighting the miners, and finally fighting for the float. This transaction had to go ahead for political reasons, and it appeared that the leading Australian funds felt they had an opportunity to exercise some power. This power had increased as capital became scarce after the GFC.

Advisors and 'experts' across the board were prepared to publicly pan the float. And a hungry media invited them to join the party. The overwhelming story in October and November 2010 was that the government had got it wrong on the price range.

Portfolio Manager at Taylor Collision Global Investors Nic Seret said: 'We're not touching it because it looks expensive.'[84]

After surveying a range of fund managers and retail client advisors, financial journalist with the *Age/Sydney Morning Herald* David Symons concluded: 'Sophisticated investors reckon the price range is just too expensive.'[85]

Mike Mangan at 2MG Asset Management added more colour: 'Repricing certainly should happen because the original price range was silly. I would look at it at $2.'[84]

Mangan added fuel to this fire by ultimately calling for the Australian Securities and Investments Commission to ban the float, claiming unfair terms for retail investors.[86]

By early November, some were confidently predicting that the Treasurer would succumb to the pressure and re-price the bid. According to *Courier Mail* journalist Tony Grant-Taylor, an 'experienced broker' expected the Treasurer to drop the price 'because he didn't want a Myer-style crash in the post-float share price.'

'He could come out and say, "We've fully tested the market and now believe $2.30 is more realistic."'.[87]

An opinion piece by David Symons on 3 November summed up the strategy of the domestic players.

'Given the feedback that has been coming in from institutions – with many indicating they will be bidding below $2.50 even if a repricing is not announced – a reduction to the bookbuild range is a near certainty. Expect that news to be released in the middle of next week.'[88]

A week later, Symons was sounding less confident, after a briefing by bankers who had witnessed the enthusiasm of overseas investors for the float.

'If the US parties bid strongly .... a repricing of the float may not be required,' he conceded.[89]

A little-known boutique advisory firm from Queensland, Hunter Green, then stepped on to the national media stage. Charlie Green featured prominently in much financial media coverage of the final stages of the float.

When the JLMs launched a counter-offensive to allay doubts over the QRN valuation assumptions, *The Australian Financial Review*'s Street Talk column mused that 'best-placed phone calls would be to Hunter Green's Charlie Green and other investors who are daring to challenge the QR juggernaut.'[90]

Age/Sydney Morning Herald columnist Ian Verrender was also sceptical about the JLM message. On 9 November, in his Fairfax syndicated column, Verrender dismissed the stories of overseas interest as too good to be true, noting that 'an air of desperation has entered proceedings'.[91]

'It's clear that on the domestic front, the response from potential investors to the high-profile, hugely expensive marketing campaign has been underwhelming to say the least. That's led to some furious spin, suggesting that canny and far more sophisticated overseas investors are champing at the bit to climb aboard that freight train to fortune.'

Andrew Fraser looks back on this period with some amusement.

'In truth, it's a shallow market in Australia, and it's dominated by too few people,' Fraser says. 'The connections between them all means that they sat around in a geographic and literal circle, mostly around Sydney, and decided that this wasn't going to work. They all agreed with each other.'

Although Fraser hadn't been involved in the formal roadshow, he had held discussions with some international investors.

'During the float I would often make the point that as soon as you left Australia, and went to any other part of the world, as you turn up people reach their arms out and put their hands in front of you to warm themselves by the fire of Australia,' Fraser says.

'Wherever you talked about the prospect people would say 'this is an integrated infrastructure company that's feeding resources into growing Asian demand, where do we sign?" Yet people in Australia were coming up with ridiculous reasons as to why this would fall over.'

Lance Hockridge spent time in Sydney with domestic institutions in the days before the bookbuild concluded. However, he found it difficult to ignite anything like the interest and passion of the international investors.

Investors Mutual investment director Anton Tagliaferro told the *Australian Financial Review* on Tuesday 16 November, just three days before the wrap up of the bookbuild, that 'the government's been poorly advised' and 'we won't be looking at anything above $2.50'.[92]

Life became even harder for QRN when BHP Billiton provocatively announced on 17 November that they would leave open the option of establishing their own rail business to haul their coal in Queensland.[93]

On the same day, global stock markets dipped amid concerns about a slowdown in China, and the worsening financial crisis in Europe. The ASX dropped nearly two per cent. AFR journalists Jenny Wiggins and Mark Ludlow couldn't resist linking the market jitters with the prospects for the QRN float.

'Sinking global stockmarkets on the eve of QR National's institutional bookbuild have deepened concerns the $6 billion float may struggle to attract investors within its forecast price range,' they wrote.[94]

And a familiar opposing voice, Nick Greiner, was once again hammering QRN in an *Australian Financial Review* feature article on 18 November, two working days before the QRN market debut.

'This is a company being sold where all of its profitable customers do not respect it or like it,' Greiner said in the article. 'I think its value will come under challenge.'[95]

On Friday 19 November, *The Australian Financial Review* ran a story headed 'QR National float fails to excite', quoting a number of global fund managers who were reportedly 'reluctant to buy into QR National, citing the pricing relative to its peers and timing of the IPO as major concerns.'[96]

However, in reality, it had become clear by this time that major interest from overseas was at least sufficient to support the stock at $2.50, if not higher.

The Treasurer was resolute about not repricing the float, and he was also reluctant to agree to the $2.50 minimum price. The JLMs were feeling the pressure and launched a last minute effort to convince Fraser to agree to $2.50.

'The JLMs, many of whom had a lot at stake as well, were seeking to lowball the offer to reduce the risk from their perspective,' Fraser says. 'They were strident in their views about the need to change. In my view, I had a really clear responsibility to execute at value to the taxpayer. Making their lives easier wasn't part of the key criteria for me.'

For bankers it was just another transaction, albeit a significant one. But a few cents on the price would make a difference of hundreds of millions of dollars to the Queensland taxpayer.

On the day of the bookbuild, Friday 19 November, Fraser flew to Sydney to conclude discussions with the bankers and make a final decision on the opening price. While his flight was in the air, some of the JLMs made the media aware of their efforts to convince the Treasurer to reduce the price. Fraser was not best pleased.

'I found it utterly reprehensible, given that we were their client,' Fraser says. 'I started the meeting, with all 40 bankers in the room, by telling them that. I said what they had done was unfathomable, unprofessional, and that it had not moved me one inch, nor would anything they did or said over the coming hours. I said if anyone felt they wanted to continue to play that game, or couldn't play by those rules, then we no longer needed them. They all looked blankly at the table.'

Fraser acknowledges that some of the JLMs had acted honourably and worked hard on the transaction. But at that moment 'the actions of one or a couple of them had tainted the whole lot of them.'

At midday on Saturday 20 November, the Treasurer announced that QR National would float on 22 November at $2.45 a share for retail investors and Queenslanders, and $2.55 a share for institutions, generating $4.6 billion for the Queensland Government. The State Government would retain up to 40 per cent of the stock, with a view to selling this down in the future.

On the morning of Monday 22 November, 2010, I woke nervous but incredibly excited. The foyer of the QRN building had been transformed with multiple posters featuring a QRN front line employee. 'Today I started my own company,' said the headline. I had pushed hard for these posters to be distributed across the company in preparation for listing day. We didn't make this deadline, but they were distributed to all sites shortly after and as I travel around the company these days, I still see the poster in the most unlikely places.

The poster celebrating our float, and our employees' ownership of QRN shares, was a tough project to get up. Many in our team wanted to play it low key, mindful of the gloom they were reading in the AFR every day. 'What if the share price tanks on the first day?' I was asked repeatedly. On the day of reckoning, I wasn't sure whether it was cavalier bravado or a finely attuned antenna that had forced me to keep pushing.

QRN's board and management team gathered at the Sofitel in Brisbane to witness the company's debut on the ASX. The ASX buying and selling database was projected on to large screens. We sat nervously, with no escape option.

In the first day of trade, the price almost immediately dropped by a cent to $2.54, apparently driven by some profit-taking by retail shareholders who had of course bought at $2.45. However, within two minutes, shares were selling for $2.60. Then there was furious buying activity, with more than 470 million QRN shares, or 20 per cent of the company's register, changing hands on the first day. The stock closed up 10c at $2.65.

Mike Carter was sitting beside Lance Hockridge during the market debut for QR National.

'I said to Lance, I'm off on leave for six weeks, I think the second pig's just taken off from the runway!' Carter says.

As they had indicated they would, many Australian institutions deliberately bid below the bookbuild range, and emerged with nothing. In the end, Australian institutions captured just 20 per cent of the shares on offer, compared to close to 40 per cent for overseas institutions. This was despite some of the foreign allocation being cut back to increase the diversity of the opening share register.

As we have seen, the company's largest private shareholder on listing was TCI. First State Investments and US-based Scout Capital were also well represented.[97] During the opening day of trading in QRN stock, a number of international investors increased their shareholdings.

Many of the domestic institutions defended their decision to avoid the IPO, saying they expected the price to drop once the JLMs were no longer supporting the stock in the 'after-market' with a 6 per cent reserve shareholding known as the 'greenshoe'. On the day of the float, Street Talk, the gossip column in *The Australian Financial Review*, claimed that 'some investors are tipping the stock will trade flat to 5c higher when it lists today, but many believe they can pick it up cheaper than the issue price early next year'.[98]

This never happened. The greenshoe was not required because of strong demand from overseas investors, and after the first minutes of trading, the share price never dipped below issue price. In fact it was quite the reverse. The stock rose 16 per cent in its first week to close at $2.84. Within five months, it was trading at $3.40.

'It's a cracker,' a relieved Treasurer declared to *The Courier Mail*. 'The outcome speaks for itself.'[99]

Commentators were quick to point out how the domestic funds had been badly out-manoeuvred.

Bryan Frith, columnist at *The Australian*, wrote that the domestic funds had simply not believed the story from QRN about overseas interest.

'The locals thought it was a tactic to persuade them to participate,' Frith wrote. 'But it was the real thing.'[100]

Frith thought that if QRN had dropped in its first week of trading, the strategy of the domestic institutions would have strengthened their hand for future IPOs.

'Not only could they pick up stock at below the issue price, but it would have enabled them to assert that vendors of large IPOs need the support of the local institutions,' he wrote.

Matthew Stevens, who as we have seen judiciously followed all of the twists in this tale, turned up the heat on the local investors, noting that the 'buoyant international interest in QR National is very telling.'

'It really does look like there were just a few more international investors clamouring for a way into Queensland's coal network than there were locals choosing an early exit.'[101]

According to *The Australian Financial Review* journalist Tony Boyd, a number of the foreign investors intimated that the valuation of the coal network assets was the secret to the miscalculation by local investors.[102]

'The fact that the locals missed this is surprising, considering the coal-mining companies had an offer on the table of $5.2 billion for the below-rail assets,' Boyd wrote.

Another lesson is that the influence of the traditional financial media would appear to be fading. As with all news, progress on IPOs these days is increasingly reported in real time. Blogs, in particular global varieties, were carrying regular messages that countered the negativity of the established press in Australia.

To its credit, *The Australian Financial Review* included an editorial on 19 November that praised the courage of the Queensland Premier and Treasurer, describing them as a 'dynamic duo'. The editors however, could not resist a final emotive dig in the same column – describing the integrated QR National as a 'bad model to foster a competitive rail industry' which had created 'another rod for the competition regulator's back'.[103]

The predicted competition disaster has not eventuated. Appropriately, Andrew Fraser had the last word.

'I never wavered in my determination, but like any human being, I had times of pessimism and doubt. But history will be very kind to this transaction.'

CHAPTER EIGHTEEN

The elegance of Hahli

T he final act in the QR National privatisation saga would involve a brand new government. On Saturday 24 March 2012, Campbell Newman's Liberal-National Party team won a landslide victory over Premier Bligh, reducing the ALP to a paltry seven seats in the 89-seat unicameral Queensland parliament. It was clear that Bligh had never been able to recover politically from the government's controversial privatisation decisions.

Although the government had not exercised a day-to-day commercial influence over the rail company after the 2010 float, and had no representation on the board, its 33 per cent stake in QR National did produce an undoubted 'overhang' effect on the share price. Many would-be institutional investors were holding off until it was clear that the government's involvement was diminished, or reduced to zero. A number of existing investors was also avoiding deeper positions for the same reasons. Customers, communities, unions and competitors were never totally convinced that the government was not pulling strings behind the scenes.

Therefore, it was important that QR National played a role in helping to find a solution to the overhang. With O'Toole driving the process, the other two key figures were new commercial general manager Prue Mackenzie (ex-Credit Suisse) and company treasurer Erin Strang.

As Hockridge and O'Toole saw it, a quick and poorly targeted sale of a government stake to speculative investors would have represented a lost opportunity. Instead, the clear preference was a government sell-down that would strengthen the company's share register via a strategic placement with large scale, credible long-term investors.

Early on, Hockridge and O'Toole were also attracted by the idea of the company buying back a portion of the government's shareholding. With the overhang impact so clear, the company's balance sheet so strong, and the company's belief in its future so resolute, the business case for this investment was compelling. Hockridge made sure that the board was briefed on this potential concept, and gained its in-principle support.

Over many months, QR National worked behind the scenes with a number of investment banks to imagine a range of ideas that would attract the Government. As with any innovation effort, there were many false starts, but momentum was building. Ultimately an ingenious idea was crafted which would go on to win the government, QR National, and investment advisors a swag of financial awards, including *Asset Magazine*'s Most Innovative Deal of the Year award.

············

The Newman Government had hit the ground running, and while the QR National shareholding was not at the top of its list, dealing with it was certainly seen as a priority and an opportunity. The approach, however, would be careful and methodical. The new Queensland Treasurer Tim Nicholls had a strong legal background, and knew the value of good process, structure and competent execution.

'We took the decision that owning the shares was not for the long term for the Queensland Government,' Nicholls says. 'We had no immediate plans, but we were going to look to sell down our interest and use the proceeds to pay down debt.'

After the high drama of the privatisation and IPO, the disposal of a significant amount of the government's remaining shareholding in October 2012 was by comparison a textbook exercise in calm and measured governance. In keeping with the broader QR saga though, there would still be a hint of vaudeville and colour.

In the first few weeks of government, as you would expect, everyone wanted to meet the new decision-makers. The Treasurer, unsurprisingly, suddenly found that he was remarkably popular among would-be investors.

'I think it took a week and people started knocking at the door,' he says. 'It was the usual story – have we got a deal for you, and where can we send the paperwork? We had to establish a process to deal with it.'

Nicholls was clear from early on about the aim – to maximise value for Queenslanders.

'We didn't want a complex deal, we didn't want fancy products, we didn't want wraps, staples and bonds and all those sorts of things,' he says. 'We wanted a clean, clear exit at maximum value that gave us the ability to capture some upside.'

Ultimately, a small project group was established to make the big recommendations – the then Under-Treasurer Helen Gluer, Philip Noble from Queensland Treasury Corporation, and ex-investment banker and new Director-General of Premier and Cabinet Jon Grayson. The group reported to the Treasurer, with the Treasurer and the Premier given final authority to make decisions. Rothschild was appointed as an external advisor.

Rather obscurely, the process was anointed as Project Hahli.

'It's a toy of one of the Under Treasurer's children – a Lego bionicle creature,' Nicholls says. '(Naming these projects) is one of the privileges of being Under-Treasurer. I would probably have called it Project Thomas.'

Nicholls had to battle a mind-set in some corners that hadn't moved on from when QR National was in full government ownership.

'I think there was still a mindset among the bureaucracy that it doesn't matter what we do or say to the directors of Aurizon, or the executive team at Aurizon, because they're still us,' he says.

'We had to be very careful in terms of our discussions with the executives and board of Aurizon, so that they understood we were acting in the best interests of the shareholders, and they were acting according to their fiduciary responsibilities in the best interests of the company. So we were very conscious of those sensitivities.'

The size of the government's stake significantly increased the sensitivity. And just as the market had tried to force the Bligh Government's hand during the float process, there was now a concerted effort to do the same with the new government.

'We were conscious that in holding such a large share, we were in a very responsible position,' Nicholls says. 'We were aware that there were certain people who were thinking that we might sell within a couple of weeks of being elected because we were strapped for cash, because of the debt situation we had been left, so we would immediately move. So they were shorting us.'

As it turned out, the government was indeed 'strapped for cash'. The softening resources boom had eroded Queensland's revenue base, but at the same time, expenditure had risen to unsustainable levels. Upon winning office, the government appointed former Federal Treasurer Peter Costello to run a Commission of Audit to examine the State's financial health. It would ultimately recommend a series of major cuts to the public service, which had grown significantly under the Beattie and Bligh Governments.

Nicholls had to resist the inclination to take the first opportunity that came along. In an extraordinary exercise in methodical analysis and patience, the government spent the best part of a year weighing up its options. In the QR National offices, we of course accepted that it was the government's prerogative to choose its own timing.

Some time after the election, Guy Fowler and Nick Brown from UBS approached the Treasurer with a particularly intriguing idea. Fowler proposed that the government reduce its stake in QR National by a half, via a combination of a QR National share buyback and investment from a brace of high calibre cornerstone investors.

'The original proposal was a $500 million buyback and a $1 billion placement,' Nicholls says. 'That required four cornerstone investors at $250 million each. That was a very attractive proposal to us. We were going down that path, but then I think a couple of the cornerstones pulled out. It was harder to execute because of the size of the placement. $1 billion was a big chunk.'

The buy-back/cornerstone idea had a real element of surprise. Most market pundits expected the government to execute a traditional on market sale, at the traditional discount to the market price. The government wanted to maximise its price for its first tranche, but also wanted to ensure its remaining shares would also be positioned for an up-lift. The UBS model offered them that promise.

'We knew that there had been a substantial amount of shorting in the month before we got there,' Nicholls says. 'Our aim in that sense was to ensure we still had hungry funds out there who still needed the weight of QR shares. So we didn't want to see it widely dispersed. We were very comfortable when UBS told us that the share buyback was a significant component and that we had cornerstones to take the big chunks.'

A month later, UBS was back at Treasury, this time with the flip of the original idea. The package would now involve a $1 billion QR National buyback, with some $500 million worth of shares allocated to cornerstones. The only trouble was that the Treasurer was on an overseas holiday with his thirteen-year-old son. Scribes would ultimately have fun with the fact that the conservative Treasurer of Queensland was in the hedonistic centre of gambling, Las Vegas.

'I was overseas with my son taking a break and we ended up in Las Vegas,' Nicholls says. 'I've always regretted that part of the story! Just stepped off a plane from Vegas, snake eyes and a cowboy hat. The real reason we were going to Las Vegas was to see the Grand Canyon.'

'The worst part about it is we got to Vegas, and Obama was in town preparing for his first Presidential debate, so they cut down all the unessential air travel. But we still managed to get a helicopter tour into the Canyon.'

Warned that something significant was brewing, Nicholls and his son were soon on a plane back to Brisbane.

'We got off the plane on Friday 5 October – we'd flown overnight, economy, no sleep,' Nicholls says. 'Within a couple of hours of getting home, I got a phone call from the Under Treasurer saying that the offer had been changed, and that it looked like a pretty good offer. I gave her authority to proceed and we had to bring people together.'

Although nothing could have prepared Nicholls for the surreal nature of doing such a large deal 'over a weekend', the team was as prepared as they could be. The government had made a point of ensuring that, at any time, all due diligence was up to date and that there were no outstanding conflicts. The process had included a 'sweep' through all departments to double-check documents and involvements with QR National. Anything potentially price-sensitive was identified and examined.

'For example, a right to build a railway line, a right to operate a port, market intelligence about a pending contract, any of those sorts of things,' Nicholls says. 'We had to satisfy ourselves and then satisfy the probity auditor that we weren't trading on the basis of knowledge we had that was not generally available in the market.'

Nicholls knew that the nature of stock markets meant that any move would need to be made after market close on Friday and before trade re-opened on a Monday. But it quickly became clear that this was going to be a particularly difficult weekend. It was the end of the school holidays, and key members of the team were dispersed across the State. Philip Noble was at the Sunshine Coast, Richard Sommerville was fishing up at Fraser Island with his children, and Bruce MacDiarmid from Rothschilds was in transit coming back from holidays.

Despite the challenges, the group pressed ahead. By Saturday 6 October, Nicholls had the full report from Rothschild on the value of the deal, an analysis of how the proposed price compared with the stock's historical performance (the volume weighted average price) and the expected effect on the market.

Nicholls spent Saturday afternoon conferring with the Hahli team, examining the Rothschild advice, and considering written advice from the Queensland Treasury Corporation. At around 6 pm, Nicholls joined a phone hookup with the Chair of QTC, Under Treasurer Gerard Bradley, Philip Noble, and Bruce McDiarmid.

'I had a number of questions and sought assurances on a couple of things,' Nicholls says. 'I was satisfied on those, and gave them the approval. I had to type on my iPad a semi-legal type of authority, I, Timothy Nicholls, Treasurer of Queensland, hereby authorise Queensland Treasury Corporation Holdings to do a transaction on the following terms. I had to cut and paste one from the other, sign it and that was the authority they needed to proceed with the deal.'

On Sunday 7 October, teams worked frenetically to prepare all the final paperwork. Their efforts were complicated by the fact that the power kept cutting in and out at the government's Executive Building, forcing people to go from floor to floor in search of a photocopier that was working. Eventually, the complete set was ready, and all negotiated changes had been made.

By this time, the Treasurer was re-connecting with his family, having been away for two weeks.

'Life doesn't stop – I took the call while I was operating my $49 Aldi spit roaster,' Nicholls says. 'My hands were covered in Moroccan spice and I was patting it on the outside of the chooks. The phone call came through and I'm scraping the spice off, and Gerard's saying "I think we've done the deal so can we have the final go-ahead". I said yes, proceed to execution and go for it. I can remember thinking – the life of a Queensland Treasurer. Within 48 hours you've gone from holidays to one of the biggest deals of the year.'

On Monday 8 October 2012, the Government surprised the market by selling down its shareholding from 33 to 15 per cent via a $1.5 billion buy-back and cornerstone investor placement deal. As Nicholls saw it, the sell-down worked well for all the key players. The State managed to get good value out of the shares, the company consolidated its share register, and shareholders received increased value. It was also an important signal of the government's ability.

'It showed that we were professional, that we were competent, that we understood what we were doing in this field, we had good advice and we were able to make and implement our decisions very effectively and efficiently,' Nicholls says.

Like Andrew Fraser, Tim Nicholls is now forever linked with a large railroad privatisation. It is part of his legacy. The reality of this hit home when Nicholls was enshrined in a national cartoon as the great railroad monetiser.

'There was a cartoon of me unhooking the train with the money sitting in the wagon,' he says. 'He made me a bit portly though. I guess it wouldn't be a cartoon otherwise! ... This deal will remain with me for a long time, I've got to say. It was one of the signature things that I did in the first 12 months of government.'

For Lance Hockridge, the deal was a vital circuit-breaker. It took advantage of the company's balance sheet for what he believed was a sensible solid investment for shareholders. And the company had diversified its shareholder base by attracting two additional high-calibre, long-term investors.

'The key thing in my mind, however, is that it represented the end of the government era for our company,' Hockridge says. 'So in that respect, it was worth an extra celebration.'

CHAPTER NINETEEN

A calm determination to change

At its heart, the successful privatisation of QR National/Aurizon is a story about change – how to construct a compelling vision, how to take your opportunities, and how to deal with setbacks and intense provocation. Lance Hockridge and his team managed change on multiple fronts; from the constant challenge of reading the motivations of senior politicians, through to the counter-intuitive battle against the express wishes of our major customers.

The pre-eminent change challenge, however, has been to transform the working culture of thousands of employees whose behaviour and choices will ultimately decide the future success of the company.

The old QR could boast many highly skilled people who wanted to do a worthwhile job. It was also home to many who had a strong sense of entitlement, and believed the company owed them a living, and indeed a 'job for life'. Inefficiencies were tolerated or ignored. Materials would mysteriously disappear regularly from storerooms.

The fuzzy reporting lines encouraged a culture of 'optionality' – where employees always felt they had the option of refusing to comply with instructions from management. With a high turnover in management ranks, many railway veterans thought they could just 'wait out' any new requirements, any new manager and any new CEO. Until the appearance of Hockridge, they had been proved right every time.

For Lance Hockridge, the philosophy has been very simple, and has not altered significantly from BHP to Bluescope to QR National/Aurizon. Successful change is about leadership, a relentless commitment to safety, and clarity of purpose.

'It really all comes down to the leaders,' Hockridge says. 'Looking back, it's interesting that people were saying to me two years after I started at QR that I hadn't done anything so perhaps it was time for new leadership. Hopefully we've made up for that since.'

Of course not every organisation requires major change-out in leadership ranks, but QR National was one that did.

'There was a clear understanding that doing more of the same wasn't going to lead to a different outcome,' he says. 'That's not a criticism of any of the people that were here in terms of capability. But for these exercises you need a certain field of experience. So the first key for change is to collect the leadership you need.'

He believes that safety matters in every organisation, from the most white-collar organisation to heavy industry. He is all too aware of the fact that eleven people have died on his watch – during his tenures at BHP, Bluescope and QR National/Aurizon.

'It becomes like a pebble in a pond, where the only way you can address it, to ensure it never happens again, is by starting at the other end and stopping all injuries,' he says. 'Because if you are not having injuries, then you're not having any fatalities.'

Hockridge supports the risk-based approaches to safety that systematically assess the circumstances that could lead to injury. But this can only ever be part of the answer.

'I just don't believe that it's possible to design enough safeguards to guard against every possible set of circumstances,' he says. 'So the key is to influence behaviour, and everyone's personal beliefs about safety. It can be done. You look at a large chemical company like Du Pont and the incredible job they do, and you realise that all injuries are indeed preventable.'

One of Hockridge's first moves was to appoint Du Pont to design a formal program of safety improvement. Over several years, a powerful new safety culture was created in the company, with responsibility and ownership moving progressively to teams and individuals. Today visitors remark on the consistency of the 'obsessive' approach to safety they see in every part of the company.

The safety strategy has fuelled a dramatic turnaround in safety performance. Lost time injury frequency rate (LTIFR), which measures the number of injuries that cause lost time per million hours worked, has fallen from 11.43 in the 2009 financial year, to 0.28 for the 2014 financial year. By this measure, Australia's biggest railroad has become if not the safest in the world, at least one of the safest.

It is perhaps not surprising that a man who studied psychology and industrial relations would end up at the helm of some extremely complex changes, in highly charged and emotional circumstances. The steel and rail industries have remarkable similarities – including employment connections that go back many generations.

'There were people at the Newcastle steelworks who were fourth generation steel workers,' he says. 'It was similar at Port Kembla, although that operation only started in the 1930s.'

'I still regularly communicate with a number of those guys. They had the most incredible emotional attachment to their jobs and their business. Despite what you hear about some people in these companies, the vast majority want to see their businesses succeed. And it's always been important to me to give these guys the respect they deserve.'

Hockridge has found the same dynamic at QR National/Aurizon. People who want their company to succeed, and see a connection between this success and their own futures.

'It means that when we talk about the need to be commercial it makes real sense,' he says. 'As I've said, many people have told me their biggest goal in life was to ensure there are good jobs for their kids and grandkids. So to the extent that that means being able to stand up and compete, then that's what we have to do.'

According to Hockridge, the final ingredient for a successful change is clarity of purpose. And like the message about competition and opportunity, it must be a shared purpose.

In January 2008, just months after starting as CEO, he wrote a long letter to managers setting out his view of the key pillars for the company, and what success would look like for the first year. He set very clear goals for improvement in safety, customer service and commercial capability. And provided a clear picture of the way he expected the organisation to be designed to deliver on these goals.

'You really can't expect people to change, certainly not to change fundamentally, without providing context and purpose,' he says. 'Why do we have this fear that people don't have the wherewithal to absorb that context and purpose and make up their own minds?'

Hockridge remembers arriving at Rockhampton during the privatisation debate on a morning when the workshop employees had been prevailed upon to go out on strike. Yet they still came back in to listen to what he had to say.

'These weren't always comfortable meetings to say the least, but the vast bulk of people turned up,' he recalls. 'A lot of them yelled at us, but a lot of them listened as well.'

The regular roadshows around the company have become a feature of his communication style. He speaks briefly to provide context and then opens the floor to questions. And while in the early days the rooms were pretty quiet, when employees started hearing unvarnished answers to direct questions, the dynamic began to change.

When the new organisation was being bedded down, we launched a process which reached more than 3,000 employees, across Australia. Based on employee feedback before the float, Hockridge established a vision for the company – 'grow our people, grow with our customers, grow the nation.' The specifics that went with this were typically bold – QR National's goal was to double the value of the company every five years. This was a company that was unequivocally about growth.

Included in the messages about the new company was a CEO promise to employees: We are building a diverse, collaborative, and creative workforce where people know what they are accountable to do and can count on having what they need to succeed.

'I know some people might think this sounds corny, but it's important, and it means we are straight with people. I would say early on, "Look, I don't expect you will always necessarily believe me, certainly you won't always like what you hear, but over time you'll be able to judge whether I and the management at this place have been telling the truth." And I think a lot of employees have seen that.'

While the organisation is no Google or Apple, it has become more collaborative. Innovation campaigns on critical safety issues have involved diverse groups from around the company. More recently, this methodology has been adapted by Glen Barber's team to encourage front line ideas to improve the bottom line, as the company seeks to reduce its operating ratio to 75 per cent (a 25 per cent EBIT margin). The 'Drive to 75' has become a company-wide movement with significant momentum. As with earlier innovation processes, the best ideas have come from the front line.

'These are real people, who've got a very clear view of what's important,' Hockridge says. 'And given the right data they have the ability to break through. There's this mind set that's infectious in old style businesses that only management knows best, and it's just not true.'

• • • • • • • • • • • •

The resourcefulness and commitment of the QR National workforce would be severely tested just weeks after the company floated in late 2010. At the end of December 2010, the company was hit with the most significant season of natural disasters Queensland had ever seen. It began with heavy rain, which resulted in flooding across an area larger than France and Germany combined. And then at the end of January 2011, a Category 5 cyclone tore through North Queensland. These two natural disasters would kill more than 30 Queenslanders.

With Hockridge on leave, Martin Moore was in the hot-seat at the time, as Acting CEO. With the heavy rain continuing for days, and then weeks, rivers swelled and reached their peaks. People were evacuated from townships in Central Queensland, in the heart of QR National's territory. Virtually all of the company's Queensland operations shut down, and in Rockhampton the flooding put the workshops underwater. But instead of cooling their heels at home, most employees were engaged in managing the emergency and the recovery, both for the business and their communities.

'We were able to mobilise people very quickly to help with the recovery,' Moore says. 'For example, our guys in Rocky RACS (Rollingstock and Component Services) of course couldn't get to work, because their site was under water. But many of them volunteered to go into the community, with their QR National orange shirts on, and help others, by getting food to them and helping them to clean up their homes and businesses.'

Despite the gravity of the crisis, Moore was proud of the company's response, and particularly the work of the people on the ground. With dangers ever present, safety performance had been exemplary.

'People were working in very difficult circumstances, where for example, there were ten times the number of snakes as normal,' Moore says. 'Despite all of that, we didn't have one lost time injury in the whole of January.'

The performance of employees in getting rail operations back up and running was extraordinary. Other than the Rolleston branch line, the main line network was reopened within weeks. While a testament to the quality of the infrastructure, it also demonstrated the powerful will of the workforce to get the network, and the State, back on its feet.

The company worked together as one with a clear single goal in mind. An operational recovery meeting was held every two days, including people from operations, maintenance and those in charge of the network. Every key operational question was thrown open to the integrated group to solve. Filling mud holes in Blackwater, for example, became less urgent because the mines in the Blackwater system were still full of water and could not operate. So instead crews were sent to Newlands, where mines were still extracting coal. In this one episode, the benefits of a vertically integrated railroad were plain for all to see.

•••••••••

While the change journey has seen many positives, of course not everything has fallen into place. For example, Hockridge and his senior team would ultimately recognise that the post-privatisation organisation structure was not going to suit the new world. In his letter to management in 2008, he called for every role to have a defined purpose, and for inter-relationships between roles to be clearly understood. To address this kind of issue, Aurizon moved away from a traditional business unit model to a functional structure which promotes excellence in key capabilities, and greater collaboration between employees.

Customer focus continues to be a challenge. In 2008, Hockridge asked managers 'How well do we know our customers, their markets and their customers? What are the economics, technologies and processes which are going to drive the demands and trends that our customers will face both in the immediate future and over the planning cycle?'

He believes QR National started a long way behind with its customers.

'Below rail, they thought we were slow, tedious to get on with, and gold-plated everything,' he says. 'We wrapped everything in such complexity that even though the headline is X, the reality is Y. And they thought we made a lot of money for zero risk. Above rail, the view was similar but overlayed by inconsistent performance, particularly in relation to our legacy contracts.'

In train operations and customer relations, it was Marcus McAuliffe who began the long process of restoring credibility, achieving real improvements in reliability and improving customer relationships. The baton was then handed to Paul Scurrah, who made the move from Queensland Rail into the QR National role of Executive Vice President Commercial and Marketing. Under Scurrah's watch, the company defied the odds to win a series of major coal contracts in Queensland and New South Wales. And with the appointment of former Vale global head of coal Mauro Neves as the new Executive Vice President of Commercial & Marketing, global expertise has now been brought in to take relationships to the next level.

The high-water-mark of this transformation was the company's success in March 2013 in winning 100 per cent of the largest coal contract of all – the 65 million tonne per year BHP Mitsubishi Alliance service in Queensland. Including innovations like supply chain performance monitoring and productivity sharing, it sent the strongest possible signal to the market. It was the largest contestable haulage contract in Australian coal in a decade, representing about a quarter of the entire Queensland coal haulage sector.

Hockridge has set the highest possible global standard for employees – the company is aiming to match or exceed the performance of the Class 1 railroads of North America.

'In the early days we had a culture of incrementalism in parts of the business,' he says. 'The objective each day was to come to work and do a good job, a bit better than yesterday and the rest takes care of itself. It's why increasingly I have been saying that the goal of this outfit is to be the equivalent of the best in the world, the Class 1 railroads. If you're going to be a bit better than the next guy, that's one thing, but if you're going to be matching it with the best in the world that's a whole other thing.'

The current Queensland Treasurer Tim Nicholls certainly believes that the company is destined to be a Class 1 railroad.

'Moving it out of the government sector has enabled it to reach a much greater potential,' Nicholls says. 'I don't think it's reached its full potential yet. It has created a business that is becoming a world-class integrated logistics organisation. In time it will match it with Burlington Northern Santa Fe and the great rail companies around the place. Over time, it has got the capacity to get there.'

Epilogue

It is now 22 November 2014. The company has just celebrated its fourth anniversary in the private sector. It is on track to keeping its market promise to double value every five years. It is poised to lead major coal and iron ore growth projects in Queensland and Western Australia, and is extending up the supply chain into bulk port operation.

The pace of change has been scorching. There is a new company name, Aurizon, and a significantly different management team. Aurizon has employed two senior Class 1 railroad executives to accelerate the transition to the performance standards of the North American railroads. Alex Kummant, formerly of Union Pacific and also for some time the CEO of the US passenger rail company Amtrak, hit the ground running in the role of Executive Vice President Strategy and is now heading up the Network business. Ex-Canadian Pacific Chief Operating Officer Mike Franczak has brought an uncompromising approach to transforming Aurizon's railroad operations as Executive Vice President Operations. As mentioned in the previous chapter, Mauro Neves, has added another dimension to customer service. The team that now leads Aurizon is diverse in its makeup and global in both its experience and outlook.

The Aurizon Board has also been further strengthened. Since IPO, new appointments include former President of Minera Alumbrera Karen Field, experienced engineer executive and director John Cooper and former Pilkington Glass Australian finance director, Pat Zito.

Changes have been logical and inevitable, as new phases of the company's history have required different skills and approaches. This does not in any way diminish the considerable achievements of the executives that have moved on, including Deb O'Toole, Marcus McAuliffe, Lindsay Cooper, Lindsay Woodland, Martin Moore, Colin Keel, Ken Lewsey, Greg Robinson and Paul Scurrah. At some stage, it will also be appropriate for a new CEO to take the helm, and Hockridge has been active in planning for his succession.

Along with the unshakeable commitment to safety, and the qualities of resilience and creativity, a lasting legacy of Aurizon's troubled birth is a corporate commitment to making difficult calls. It's critical for renewal, and ultimately building value. People are expected to perform, be rewarded appropriately, and then allow for the next stage of value to evolve, even if that means new talent driving it.

Aurizon is unique among railroad companies in that it is particularly oriented to the global view. At critical points in its development the company has been quite literally forced overseas: first, in the search for privatisation models; secondly, for international investors in the IPO; and thirdly, for world class operational models after IPO. Add to this the international experience of Prescott, Hockridge, and other key figures in the company's board and management, and you have an environment that encourages a view beyond the borders of Queensland, and Australia. In addition, Aurizon now has the financial and commercial networks that befit a potential global player. Relationships in China, North America, India and Japan are strong, and developing well in South Korea.

The health of China is important to Australia, Queensland and Aurizon. While, at the time of writing, it ranks slightly behind Japan as an end market for the coal that Aurizon hauls, it is nonetheless the emotional energy of the world economy and the price-setter for so many commodities, including coal and iron ore. Any disruption in China becomes an immediate inclusion in the questions Hockridge is asked on international investor roadshows.

The typical Western view of China is becoming increasingly out-dated. Without liberalised political and economic institutions, the theme goes, surely disaster is just around the corner? Every crisis trigger has been elucidated, elevated and elongated by the critics. For years we have been waiting for the Chinese property bubble to burst. Local instability, while real and reflected in more than 80,000 demonstrations per year requiring police intervention, has not led to a predicted implosion. China's reported go-slow on reforms to intellectual property law has not prevented an explosion in Chinese innovation, R&D, and the number of home-grown entrepreneurs.

The global obsession with China's headline GDP growth rate has led to some bizarre conclusions. A softening of annual growth to below 8 per cent in 2013 and 2014 has been interpreted as a global economic catastrophe. Yet, for Aurizon's most important end market, the steel sector, using 2013 figures as a baseline, a Chinese growth rate of just 5 per cent generates *additional* annual demand for 30 mtpa of metallurgical coal and 55 mpta of iron ore.

Aurizon's market intelligence unit and its senior executives have spent several years deepening their understanding of these global dynamics. The company's continued confidence in the Australian coal and iron ore sectors is based on extensive research and interviews with customers, analysts, economists, diplomats, bankers and fellow businesses.

All of this has set the scene for the bold growth moves that have been made by the company since privatisation. Two projects in particular have changed the game for Aurizon. The first is a proposed joint venture with the large Indian energy company GVK to build new rail and port infrastructure to expand the Northern Bowen Basin and open up Queensland vast thermal coal deposits in the Galilee Basin.

The second is an inspired takeover of mid-tier Australian iron ore mining company Aquila, again in joint venture with an offshore partner, Baosteel, one of China's largest steel producers. With the Aquila move, Aurizon's intention is not to be a long-term investor in a mining company, but to use this position to become majority owner and operator of a new rail and port corridor in the emerging West Pilbara iron ore region.

These ventures have been encouraged and shaped from the top, but importantly have been conceived and driven by two home-grown entrepreneurs,

James Moutafis, in the case of Galilee, and David Welch with the Baosteel transaction.

The broader transformation in Australia has also been significant. Australian governments are moving assertively across the board to eliminate waste and inefficiency, and withdraw subsidies and handouts that many considered were untouchable. Privatisation of essentially commercial activity is back on the agenda, where it belongs. Without doubt, we would not be seeing this extent of privatisation if, as many of the pundits predicted, the QR National float had failed.

Four years ago, in the dying days of government ownership and racked by controversy and division, it would have been hard to imagine today's picture of growth and success at Aurizon. While the company still has a long way to go, it's a good example of what can be achieved with a little bit of creativity, resilience and determination.

When complacency is finally banished from its remaining pockets of power, you can expect to see many more Aurizons created out of the quagmire of government ownership.

Watch this space.

Endnotes

1. Fast-tracked Fraser wasn't always number 1, *Brisbane Times*, 16 September 2007.
   http://www.brisbanetimes.com.au/news/queensland/fasttracked-fraser-wasnt-always-no1/2007/09/16/1189881330385.html?page=fullpage

2. Seeney blasts Fraser over council amalgamation handling, *ABC Online*,
   10 May 2007.
   http://www.abc.net.au/news/2007-05-10/seeney-blasts-fraser-over-council-amalgamation/2545014

3&4. Mayors axed in forced mergers, *The Australian*, 28 July 2007.
   http://www.theaustralian.com.au/archive/news/mayors-axed-in-forced-mergers/story-e6frg6oo-1111114056327

5. The global steel industry: innovation; restructuring; free trade, speech by
   Lance Hockridge, The American Chamber of Commerce in Australia Amcham/
   Stephens Lawyers & Consultants Business Luncheon, 17 October 2003.

6. Paul Cronin worked in the Officer of the Queensland Premier as Principal Media
   Advisor from 2005 to 2008. He worked for both Premier Beattie and Premier
   Bligh.

7. Keith De Lacy is a successful businessman and a former Labor Treasurer of
   Queensland from 1989 to 1996. One of Queensland's best-known company
   directors, he was Chair of Macarthur Coal Limited until its takeover by Peabody
   Energy in 2011.

8. Sir Leslie Thiess was a Queensland business icon. He was part of a group of brothers that establish the Thiess engineering company in the 1930s. Sir Leslie is credited with a pioneering role in open-cut coalmining, the Australia-Japan coal trade, and the Australian distribution of Toyota vehicles. The Thiess business was publicly listed in 1958 and became part of the Leighton Group in 1983. The company turns over $7 billion of work annually in construction, mining and diversified services.

9. Founded in 1924, Mount Isa Mines (MIM) operated the major copper, lead, zinc and silver mines around the Mount Isa region in Queensland. It grew into a major mining house, and for a brief period in 1980, MIM was Australia's largest company. MIM was acquired by Xstrata for $4.93 billion in 2003.

10. David Hamill was Treasurer of Queensland from 1998 until his retirement from Parliament in 2001. He represented the Ipswich electorate as its MP from 1983 until 2001. He is now a director of several corporations and NGOs.

11. Interail was created out of QR's purchase of Northern Rivers Railroad, which added standard gauge locomotives and wagons to the QR fleet.

12. Based at Altona in Melbourne, CRT was built from humble beginnings by the Rees family into a significant logistics business with an annual turnover of $80 million and 250 employees. Its acquisition by QR added a significant fleet of trucks, rollingstock and terminals in key locations, as well as a specialist capability in the transport of polymer and food products.

13. The Australian Railroad Group sale in February 2006 created a vertically separated structure out of a formerly vertically-integrated railroad. ARG's joint venture partners Wesfarmers and Genesee & Wyoming sold the track infrastructure to Babcock and Brown and the rail haulage business to QR. The total sale price was $1.3 billion.

14. Stephen O'Donnell was CEO of Pacific National from February 2002 to October 2005. Previously he was Executive General Manager Australian Smelting with the diversified Australian mining company Pasminco.

15. O'Donnell review puts cost of Goonyella losses at $1 bn, *Lloyds List DCN*, 31 July 2007.
    http://www.railexpress.com.au/archive/2007/Jul/26/odonnell-review-puts-cost-of-goonyella-losses-at-1bn

16. Anna Bligh was the first woman to be appointed Premier of Queensland. She held the role from September 2007 to March 2012. She was previously Deputy Premier and Treasurer in the Beattie Government.

17. Ken Lewsey has a background in logistics, steel and mining services. In additional to Brambles, he held senior leadership roles with BHP Steel, Cleanaway and Smorgon Steel. He is currently CEO of mining services company Emeco.

18. Greg Pringle was previously Group Company Secretary for Flight Centre Limited, and a strategic management consultant with PwC. His legal career included a period as a magistrate in South Africa.

19. Martin Moore was Chief Information Officer at MIM and National Transport Insurance. He later served as General Manager Strategy for NTI. He is currently CEO of the Queensland power company CS Energy.

20. Queensland Rail's 'gravy plane' tour cost $45,000, *The Courier-Mail* 1 May 2008.
http://www.couriermail.com.au/news/queensland/gravy-plane-bill-cost-15k/story-e6freoof-1111116209332

21. Matt Keenan is now Managing Director of the corporate advisory business with Gresham Partners, an independent Australian investment and advisory group. He was previously Head of Transport and Infrastructure within the Investment Banking division of Merrill Lynch.

22. Robin Franklin had held senior executive positions with BP Australia Ltd, MIM Holdings Limited and Thiess Contractors Pty Ltd. After his involvement in the 2009 EBA negotiations, he took on the role of Director of the Integration Management Office for the establishment of the separated government railway Queensland Rail in 2010.

23. Originally from Scotland, Owen Doogan is a long-term railway union operative. He joined the forerunner of the Rail Tram and Bus Union, the Australian Railways Union, as Industrial Officer in 1991.

24. *The Pig That Flew*, Harry Bruce, Douglas & McIntyre, 1997.

25. Secret behind Anna Bligh's Queensland election victory, *The Sunday Mail*, 22 March 2009.
http://www.couriermail.com.au/news/special-features/secret-behind-blighs-victory/story-e6freoqx-1225698241881

26. Renewing Queensland: Future Investment Plan, Media Statement by Premier and Minister for the Arts, The Honourable Anna Bligh, and Treasurer and Minister for Employment and Economic Development, The Honourable Andrew Fraser, 2 June 2009.
http://statements.qld.gov.au/Statement/Id/64177

27. State power sends bills sky high, Annabel Hepworth, *The Australian*, 23 May 2011.
http://www.theaustralian.com.au/national-affairs/state-power-sends-bills-sky-high/story-fn59niix-1226060718591

28. Iemma must stand firm on privatisation push: Kennett, *The World Today,* 5 May 2008.
http://www.abc.net.au/worldtoday/content/2008/s2235591.htm
https://www.coag.gov.au/node/52

29. Competition Principles Agreement, 11 April 1995.
https://www.coag.gov.au/node/52

30. Regulatory and competition policy context for rail privatisation in Queensland, a report prepared for Queensland Rail, Professor Allan Fels AO, September 2009.

31. Additional observations on competition policy in the context of the Queensland coal systems, A follow-up paper prepared for Queensland Rail, Professor Allan Fels, October 2009.

32. The Queensland Government developed seven criteria to guide the decision on the best privatisation model for QR National:
    1. Maximising sales proceeds;
    2. Minimising residual government risk;
    3. Facilitating private sector provision of infrastructure;
    4. Creating sustainable businesses;
    5. Minimising execution risk;
    6. Optimising infrastructure;
    7. Promoting above rail competition.
33. QR given maximum fine, *The Australian Financial Review*, 23 June 2010.
34. QR's great split a logistical nightmare, *The Australian Financial Review*, 3 May 2010.
35. Bligh runs state off the rails, Matthew Stevens, *The Australian*, 10 December 2009.
    http://www.theaustralian.com.au/business/opinion/bligh-is-runs-state-off-the-rails/story-e6frg9if-1225808806118
36. BHP behind bid to buy QR, Matthew Stevens, *The Australian*, 16 December 2009.
37. BHP's Qld Rail offer rebuffed, Mark Ludlow, *The Australian Financial Review*, 18 December 2009.
38. Queensland privatisation backlash widens, Mark Ludlow, *The Australian Financial Review*, 10 December 2009.
39. BHP behind bid to buy QR, Matthew Stevens, *The Australian*, 16 December 2009.
40. Miners bid for slice of QR sale, Matthew Stevens, *The Australian*, 12 December 2009.
41. The Queensland Competition Authority has economic regulatory responsibility for Queensland's rail, water and power sectors. It was established by the Queensland Government in 1997 as part of the implementation of the national competition policy agreed by the Council of Australian Governments.
42. Ferguson quietly backs Greiner, Matthew Stevens, *The Australian*, 17 March 2010.
43. Queensland Government slammed for proposed coal haulage sale, *The 7.30 Report*, ABC TV, 24 March 2010.
    http://www.abc.net.au/7.30/content/2010/s2855262.htm
44. Coal miners say train privatisation plan off the rails, Andrew Fraser, *The Australian*, 26 March 2010.
45. Coal bid for QR looms – Greiner, Mark Ludlow, *The Australian Financial Review*, 5 May 2010.
46. The 0.01 per cent: the rising influence of vested interests in Australia, Wayne Swan, *The Monthly*, March 2012.
    https://www.themonthly.com.au/issue/2012/march/1344425290/wayne-swan/001-cent-rising-influence-vested-interests-australia
47. Premier's sell-off boosts efficiency, Michael Stutchbury, *The Australian*, 9 December 2009.

48. However you spin it, it's privatisation, Mark Ludlow, *The Australian Financial Review*, 9 December 2009.

49. Queensland Rail float vital to fund infrastructure, Media Release, *Infrastructure Partnerships Australia*, 0 December 2009.
http://www.google.com.au/url?sa=t&rct=j&q=the%20float%20will%20allow%20queensland%20backlog%20lyon&source=web&cd=1&ved=0CB4QFjAA&url=http%3A%2F%2Finfrastructure.org.au%2FDisplayFile.aspx%3FFileID%3D320&ei=qGGmU8XYF8SGkAXD8ICQCg&usg=AFQjCNGz-1sFTQXYHIcs_DOodWO7Nn16Hg&bvm=bv.69411363,d.dGI

50. QR sale will stifle competition, Brendan Lyon, *The Australian Financial Review*, 9 February, 2010.

51. QR float bodes well for Queensland, Lance Hockridge, *The Australian Financial Review*, 11 February 2010.

52. QR must split up to be saved, Mark Christensen, *The Australian Financial Review*, 19 April 2010.

53. Prescott dismisses separation comparison to Telstra, Matthew Stevens, *The Australian*, 28 April 2010.

54. US chief warns of rail-split 'disaster', Glenda Korporaal, *The Australian*, 18 May 2010.
http://www.theaustralian.com.au/business/us-chief-warns-of-rail-split-disaster/story-e6frg8zx-1225867946850

55. Vertical integration delivers the goods, Douglas Young, *The Australian* 15 June 2010.
http://www.theaustralian.com.au/business/vertical-integration-delivers-the-goods/story-e6frg8zx-1225879641734

56. Hold onto your hats, the coal miners are coming, Street Talk, *The Australian Financial Review*, 20 May 2010.

57. Asciano move may delay QR sale, Mark Ludlow, *The Australian Financial Review*, 19 May 2010.

58. Valemus decision may kill QR rail offering, Mark Ludlow, *The Australian Financial Review*, 7 July 2010.

59. Coal firms stoke move for assets, James McCullough, *The Courier-Mail*, 16 April 2010.
http://www.news.com.au/national/coal-firms-stoke-move-for-assets/story-e6frfkp9-1225854734859

60. Coal miners bid $4.85 bn for Queensland rail track network, Rebecca Thurlow and Alex Wilson, *The Australian*, 26 May 2010.
http://www.theaustralian.com.au/archive/business/coal-miners-bid-485bn-for-qld-rail-track-network/story-e6frg9e6-1225871439435

61. Greiner's miners boost their bid for Queensland rail infrastructure, Matthew Stevens, *The Australian*, 10 August 2010.
http://www.theaustralian.com.au/archive/business-old/greiners-miners-boost-their-bid-for-queensland-rail-infrastructure/story-e6frg97o-1225903163774

62. Miners can't get Bligh off her track, Matthew Stevens, *The Australian*, 10 March 2010.

63. Premier admits to sell-off errors, Rosanne Barrett, *The Australian*, 8 September 2010.

64. Queensland will not be infected by the NSW corrosion, Anna Bligh says, AAP, *The Australian*, 23 August 2010.
http://www.theaustralian.com.au/national-affairs/state-politics/queensland-will-not-be-infected-by-the-nsw-corrosion-anna-bligh-says/story-e6frgczx-1225908974315

65. Coal bid threatens viability, says boss, Matthew Stevens, *The Australian*, 1 September 2010.

66. Rail disaster is the blight at the end of this tunnel, The Prince, *The Australian Financial Review*, 4 September 2010.

67. Premier on track to decide fate of QR National's privatisation, Matt Chambers and Andrew Main, *The Australian*, 9 September 2010.

68. Political backtracking on QR National signals weakness, Bob Herbert, *The Courier-Mail*, 10 September 2010.
http://www.couriermail.com.au/news/political-backtracking-on-qr-national-signals-weakness/story-e6frerdf-1225916625434

69. QR unlikely to set pulses racing for long, Criterion, Tim Boreham, *The Australian*, 12 October 2010.

70. QR bid withdrawal an embarrassment for coalminers, Matthew Stevens, *The Australian*, 10 September 2010.
http://www.theaustralian.com.au/business/opinion/qr-bid-withdrawal-an-embarrassment-for-coalminers/story-e6frg9if-1225916737456

71. Fox wary of QR National's growth forecasts, Mark Ludlow, *The Australian Financial Review*, 29 October 2010.

72. Investors warned of QR float's tax risks, Jamie Walker, *The Australian*, 11 October 2010.

73. Something to prove for rail chief, Jenny Wiggins, *The Australian Financial Review*, 13 October 2010.

74. QR National float still on track, Philip Baker, *The Australian Financial Review*, 23 October 2010.

75. All aboard for the QR ride, Liam Walsh, *The Courier-Mail*, 11 September 2010.

76. Listing just the driver QR would want, *The Australian Financial Review*, 29 October 2010.

77. QR National: not enough engine to climb the hill, Ian Verrender, *The Age*, 9 November 2010.

78. Overseas interest strong for rail float, Alex Tilbury, *The Courier-Mail*, 19 November 2010.

79. Quick buck on QRN float doubtful, Alex Tilbury, *The Courier-Mail*, 20 November 2010.

80. Prescott dismisses separation comparison to Telstra, Matthew Stevens, *The Australian*, 28 April 2010.

81. Less than compelling offer, Anthony MacDonald, *The Australian Financial Review*, 25 October 2010.

82. Asciano guns for QR National business, Jenny Wiggins, *The Australian Financial Review*, 1 December 2010.
83. Being part of something big could be a hard concept to sell, Paddy Manning G-Biz, *The Age*, 25 September 2010.
84. Investors demand pledge Queensland won't play trains with QR National, Jenny Wiggins, Mark Ludlow and Gillian Tan, *The Australian Financial Review*, 6 November 2010.
85. High hopes, David Symons, *Sydney Morning Herald*, 29 October 2010.
86. QR Nat float is off track, say analysts, Tony Grant-Taylor, *The Courier-Mail*, 19 October 2010.
87. D-Day for rail investors to jump aboard, Tony Grant-Taylor, *The Courier-Mail*, 6 November 2010.
88. QR valuation pulls up a bit short of platform, David Symons, *The Age*, 3 November 2010.
89. QR spruikers feel love from America, David Symons, *The Age*, 10 November 2010.
90. Doubts about QR debt set damage control in train, Street Talk, *The Australian Financial Review*, 5 November 2010.
91. QR National: not enough engine to climb the hill, Ian Verrender, *The Age*, 9 November 2010.
92. QR on whistle-stop tour of investors, Mark Ludlow, Jenny Wiggins and Gillian Tan, *The Australian Financial Review*, 16 November 2010.
93. BHP may derail QRN with network, Alex Tilbury, *The Courier-Mail*, 18 November 2010.
94. Tanking markets test QR bookbuild, Jenny Wiggins and Mark Ludlow, *The Australian Financial Review*, 18 November 2010.
95. Interview with Nick Greiner, *The Australian Financial Review*, 18 November 2010.
96. QR National float fails to excite, Gillian Tan, *The Australian Financial Review*, 19 November 2010.
97. NY hedge fund scoops up a chunk of QR, Jenny Wiggins, *The Australian Financial Review*, 25 November 2010.
98. Greenshoe could work its magic on QR National, Street Talk, *The Australian Financial Review*, 22 November 2010.
99. Investors smiling as QR National returns steam ahead, James McCullough, *The Courier-Mail*, 27 November 2010.
100. Railway's successful debut may restore investor faith in IPOs, Bryan Frith, *The Australian*, 23 November 2010.
101. It's all aboard for overseas investors, Matthew Stevens, *The Australian*, 23 November 2010.
102. QR float leaves locals trackside, Chanticleer, Tony Boyd, *The Australian Financial Review*, 23 November 2010.
103. Praise for some rare government courage, Editorial, *The Australian Financial Review*, 19 November 2010.

Index

ACKNOWLEDGMENTS

I am indebted to the many people from both business and government communities that graciously agreed to be interviewed for this book. I need to make particular mention of Aurizon Chair John Prescott, Aurizon CEO Lance Hockridge, former Queensland treasurer Andrew Fraser, and former Canadian Transport Minister Doug Young. They were extraordinarily generous with their time and insights and helped to bring this complicated and intriguing story to life.

Thank you to my wonderful wife, Suzy, who suggested the idea, and then provided encouragement at every step of the way.

Thanks to Gresham's Matt Keenan for adding a crucial insiders' perspective, and putting up with my continual fact-checking questions. Thanks also to Catherine Taggart, who made sure that key events and dates were as accurate as possible, and to Mark O'Connor from Aurizon's legal team for his meticulous work with the continually changing manuscript!

My sincere thanks to Ken Wiltshire, who has had an interest in our story for many years and introduced me to the University of Queensland Press. UQP have been fantastic, in particular Lynn Bryan, who understood early on what I was trying to achieve and moved heaven and earth to make it happen. I am also grateful to editor Janet Hutchinson, who made invaluable suggestions for improvement when they were needed most.